INSIGHT vs. DESENSITIZATION IN PSYCHOTHERAPY

INSIGHT vs. DESENSITIZATION IN PSYCHOTHERAPY

An Experiment in Anxiety Reduction

GORDON L. PAUL

1966
STANFORD UNIVERSITY PRESS
STANFORD CALIFORNIA

To Joan

ACKNOWLEDGMENTS

This monograph is based on my doctoral dissertation in psychology for the University of Illinois. I wish to express thanks to my adviser, Charles W. Eriksen, and the members of my doctoral committee, Wesley C. Becker, Lloyd G. Humphreys, Merle M. Ohlsen, Donald T. Shannon, and Jerry S. Wiggins, for their valuable suggestions and continuing support. Thanks are also extended to the participating therapists, observers, and clerical workers whose diligence made this study possible.

Appreciation is expressed to the staff of WILL-TV for providing facilities for training observers, and to Karl R. Wallace and the participating instructors of the Speech Department for allowing the use of class time for testing and for handling test batteries. A special note of thanks goes to Severina Nelson for her invaluable coordination of classroom procedures, and to Ted J. Barnes and Thomas M. Scheidel for their suggestions on speech conditions.

Finally, I am grateful to my wife, Joan M. Paul, for the long hours of work she so willingly donated, and to my children, Dennis, Dana, and Joni, for their understanding and cooperation during the extended period of time in which I was absorbed in this project.

The research reported herein was supported in part by Fellowship No. 1 Fl MH-19, 873-01, from the National Institute of Mental Health, Public Health Service, and in part by the Cooperative Research Program of the Office of Education, U.S. Department of Health, Education, and Welfare, Contract No. 4-10-080, Project S-006.

November 1965   G. L. P.

CONTENTS

INSIGHT vs. DESENSITIZATION IN PSYCHOTHERAPY

INTRODUCTION AND PROBLEM

In recent years there has been a growing controversy over the relative merit of "insight" and "behavioral" treatments in the field of psychotherapy. Although active, direct intervention into maladaptive behaviors and emotions actually predated today's traditional psychotherapeutic approach (James 1915), the overwhelming impact of Freudian theory readily displaced the older, unsystematic re-educative procedures. Insight therapy became standard.

Since Freud's time, there have been many innovations in the theory and technique of psychotherapy, including the translation of Freudian theory into learning terms (as in Shoben 1949, Dollard and Miller 1950), and the rise of eclecticism and other schools. It was not until 1952, with the publication of Eysenck's provocative review article, that the efficacy of traditional psychotherapy (or of any psychotherapy at all) was seriously questioned. Since then, direct attacks on the "disease model" of psychopathology (Szasz 1961) and on the value of insight per se (Hobbs 1962) have become more vehement. Although fairly systematic methods of behavioral retraining, or emotional re-education, based on a "learning model" have been in existence for some time (for example, Jones 1924), true proponents of these methods, such as Bachrach, Bandura, Eysenck, and Wolpe, have emerged only recently. Extremists on both sides have not hesitated to discredit each other, even though well-controlled comparative studies are nonexistent.

Problems of Outcome Research

The problems and complexities of research in psychotherapy, or behavior modification, have been the focus of two national conferences held by the American Psychological Association (Rubinstein and Parloff 1959, Strupp and Luborsky 1962); the current state of affairs in the area can be characterized by Colby's (1964) statement, "Chaos prevails." This chaotic condition appears to result from the formidable methodological and control problems, as emphasized by Frank (1959a), and from the lack of a feasible model for outcome research. Of course, there is little disagreement about the basic design of an outcome study that involves measurement of a subject's cognitive, physiological, or motoric behavior: it should include pretreatment and posttreatment phases and appropriate control groups. Beyond that, the diffiulties begin. The lack of solid empirical evidence makes even selection of controls less precise than desirable, and many variables that intuitively seem necessary to control are themselves researchable areas.

The first problem in constructing an outcome study is to reach an adequate definition of the sample. Ideally, the criteria used should be clear and precise enough to make near-duplication possible. At the same time, they must be relevant to the goals of treatment. None of the customary definitional criteria are adequate in these respects. Actuarial characteristics are easily attainable, but far from sufficient. The major interest in defining the sample is perhaps the clinical diagnosis, which unfortunately is usually based upon vague and overlapping criteria.

Frank suggests two approaches that might be possible within the limitations of the conventional diagnostic scheme. The first of these is the characterization of subjects in terms of motivations and conflicts, with goals determined for each subject uniquely. Unfortunately such classifications are based on inferences that depend to a great extent on the researcher's theoretical preconceptions, thus increasing the unreliability of classification. The second possibility appears more promising. This approach involves the selection and description of subjects in terms of "target behaviors," with the goal of treatment being to change these behaviors in a specific direction. With this approach, ability to replicate the sample is more assured, and measurement of outcome more focused.

There are some purely practical problems involved in defining the sample: obtaining a large enough sample to adequately test the efficacy of techniques, gaining adequate information on the subjects prior to treatment assignment, and finding adequate time for appraisal. After selecting and describing the sample, the next problem is dividing it into treatment and control groups. There are conceivably four ways of doing this. One way (existing only in fantasy) is to match the individual subjects in all respects, so that each group is the perfect equivalent of every other group. A second method is to match groups on the major variables believed to be significant, such as target behaviors, motivation, age, and sex, randomizing other aspects. Because of practical limitations, this is next to impossible in clinic field studies, since each additional matching variable greatly increases the size of the population to be screened. This approach is more reasonable, however, in settings such as hospitals, prisons, and universities, where one has a captive population. A third possibility is to match groups by stratified sampling of major categories, without matching individuals. This method is often too cumbersome for clinics, although possible if one extends the project over a long period of time or draws on several clinic populations. This procedure should be possible with one of the "captive" populations mentioned above. The fourth method is straight random assignment. For any method of assignment, randomization of those variables not matched is important; and one should be careful to check whether or not randomization has achieved its objective. In experimental studies the very least that should be attempted would seem to be stratification on target behaviors and motivation. Of course, the more homogeneous the original selection, the more equivalent any method of assignment to groups will be.

In the past, the use of each subject as his own control has been used in an attempt to circumvent problems of control groups. Own-control designs are desirable for obtaining base rates with which one can compare behavioral changes following treatment, but they do not eliminate the problems imposed by withholding treatment, nor do they adequately control changes related to the passage of time, season, and intercurrent life experiences. There is no alternative to including comparable groups. Again, the practical problems met in defining the sample are present, i.e., obtaining a large enough sample, accumulating prior information, and, in this particular case, dealing with the problems surrounding the withholding of treatments for no-treatment control groups.

Situational variables, which include the therapist, the therapeutic circumstances, therapist-subject interaction, and external environment, pose even greater control problems. The first task of situational control should be to provide for the eventuality that the behavioral modifications which may be observed are not due to intercurrent life experiences or spontaneous fluctuations within the subjects. The latter is particularly important in "in vivo" studies, since a client is most apt to seek treatment when he is worst off, with no direction to move except toward improvement. Also, if the treatment involves children, growth and maturation may contribute to observed behavioral changes. Once again, the obvious way of controlling for these factors is to use a comparable no-treatment control group that is observed for the same amount of time as the treatment groups.

In hospital settings, the life experience of patients can theoretically be controlled, although the practical difficulties of gaining administrative support are formidable. Clinic field studies also present real difficulties. For instance, subjects placed on waiting lists are usually quite different from those immediately accepted. Refusal to admit clients to treatment is often seen as rejection, thus changing the population in some respects: the subjects in the no-treatment group tend to drop out or seek treatment elsewhere. When complete control is not available, assessing these possibilities after the fact is a necessary compromise. Some obvious controls can be attempted in working with students, although the practical problems, even with a captive population, at times seem insurmountable.

One suggestion that Frank makes is to offer differing types of treatment to a control group. This is of course useful in some instances, but no substitute for the no-treatment control. To compare the relative efficacy of different therapeutic techniques, one ought to pay particular attention to keeping the amount of contact (i.e., length and number of sessions) and the spacing of sessions constant.

A further control, which is an absolute necessity for outcome studies in which the efficacy of a specific technique is to be evaluated, is control of what Rosenthal and Frank (1958) have termed the "placebo effect." The placebo effect in psychotherapy refers to behavioral changes arising from the nonspecific aspects of attention, suggestion, and faith (in the therapist and his techniques) that are common to most such interpersonal situations. In fact, Frank (1959b) implies that the placebo effect may be the basic determinant of a therapist's influence. An adequate control for placebo effects would then be another form of "treatment" in which the subjects have equal faith, but which would not be expected to lead to behavioral change on any other grounds.

The use of no-treatment control groups presents a special problem, which is related to placebo effects. Along with Frank, Goldstein (1960) has argued that no-treatment control groups may derive so much benefit from the personal attention and positive expectancies received from interviewing, individual testing, and promise of eventual treatment that they fail to provide a true "no-treatment" group. But since a group not receiving specific treatment is an absolute necessity for certain situational factors, one must include it. Rather than considering such groups as a control for "spontaneous remission," one might better consider them as the base-rate improvement of extra-treatment contact, or perhaps as Borgotta's (1959) "Limbo-therapy." Another possibility would be the inclusion of a second minimal-contact or no-contact control group to provide at least a fractional replication of some measures. Such a control, which would of course be nearly impossible in field work relying upon client referrals for subjects, is possible in certain experimental studies.

The personal attributes of the therapist and his faith in a particular form of treatment are intimately bound up with the placebo effect in treatment. The chief problem of control in this respect is to distinguish the effects of the therapist's personality from the effects of his techniques. It is unlikely that a therapist can use different types of treatment with precisely equal skill, or that his attitudes toward them will be identical. It is difficult to control adequately for the influence of the therapist as a person when, again, so little is known about the role of his personal attributes and attitudes in determining the outcome of treatment.

Some research does suggest that therapists can effectively role-play confidence in techniques they do not necessarily have faith in (Snyder 1962). The two approaches to control of this problem seem to be either having each therapist use his preferred technique, assuming that personal attributes have entered into this choice, or having each therapist use different techniques, thereby holding personal attributes constant across groups. The use of this latter method seems most promising, particularly in conjunction with the use of placebo controls, because it gives a base rate of sorts to the improvement resulting from the personal impact and prestige of the therapist on the subjects. For this method, one must find therapists who are open-minded enough to learn to use contradictory methods without exhibiting attitudes that would greatly affect their approach. Even then it is necessary to use some after-the-fact check on the therapists, probably interviews or questionnaires.

Few studies report the qualifications, experience, and attitudes of the therapists in enough detail to show what treatment took place, much less to permit replication. Of course, in working with emotional re-education and placebo treatments, almost all therapists will be neophytes, but here, too, the training and instruction given should be as uniform as possible. It is also necessary to obtain a complete statement from each therapist on his use of various techniques, and to follow this up by sound recordings or other methods to see that the therapist is actually doing what he says he is. Simple labeling of "schools" is not enough.

Frank mentions a third major area of control difficulty, that of response variables. Here we meet the problem that has been primarily responsible for discouraging outcome studies, the criterion

problem. Any mention of the criterion problem in outcome research usually leads to a long argument about what is meant by
improvement (Bergin 1963). To my mind, the most sensible way
to advance scientific knowledge about behavior modification is to
assume that selection of subjects defines the behaviors to be assessed for change. This is especially true if subjects are selected
who exhibit specific target systems or behaviors. The goals of treatment are then relatively specific.

Although many techniques for measuring change have been
used in the past, few of these methods have proved to be accept-
able (Zax and Klein 1960). Because of individual biases, subjec-
tive reports by subjects or therapists are notorious for their lack of
validity and reliability. Subjects will often answer questions on the
basis of how they feel about undergoing treatment, or how they
like the therapist, rather than give direct responses to specific
questions; therapists often evaluate treatment outcome on subject
likability or openness instead of on more objective factors. In the
same way, obvious paper-and-pencil tests are open to deception
and less obvious tests may not be sensitive to change. Especially
in the use of projective instruments such as ink blots, the relationship to other behavior may be unknown. The latter problem also
places great restrictions on any suggested method of using intra-
therapy measures for outcome. When tests are used, controls for
mere repetition of testing are also necessary. As Zax and Klein
point out, the least used and most promising method would appear to be the use of external, objective criteria, such as blind
ratings by trained observers of external behavior. For control purposes, behavioral tests for selected target behaviors are the most
desirable because they remove the possibility of faking and bias,
factors that might be present in ratings by significant others.

Any discussion of response variables would be incomplete without mentioning the importance of follow-ups on obtained effects.
The same problems and difficulties that have been mentioned in
connection with assessing immediate effects are also relevant for
follow-up, with the use of external, objective criteria still being the
most desirable solution. Practical problems are overwhelming dur-

ing follow-up: the longer the study extends in time, the greater is the attrition of the sample. Often, attrition is selective; the handful of subjects who remain are often much different from those who made up the original sample. Perhaps the most promising approach at present is to use relatively short-term follow-ups that permit total sample assessment, because the impact of therapeutic intervention, at least with disturbances usually classified as "neurotic," may be primarily the hastening of changes that might eventually be expected to occur in the life situation alone (Frank 1961).

Anxiety, a Research Focus

Several researchers in the area have suggested discontinuing outcome studies because of the problems and difficulties involved (Strupp 1962a). Rather than discontinue outcome research, we need to find an efficient means of approaching an evaluation of the relative effectiveness and appropriate areas of application of various psychotherapeutic approaches; in this way, we might bring order to Colby's "chaos." Initially, we would have to compare specific techniques in the treatment of an emotional problem that is delimited enough to allow rigorous experimental methodology, but significant enough to allow generalization from the findings and to have implications for further study in the broader field of counseling and psychotherapy. Interpersonal-performance anxiety is such an emotional problem.

The importance of anxiety in theories of psychopathology hardly needs documentation. Anxiety is seen as the major component in most, if not all, current theories, and the reduction of anxiety is an implicit or explicit goal of every psychotherapeutic approach. Furthermore, the effects of debilitating performance anxiety on relevant behaviors appear to differ in no qualitative way from the effects produced by more widespread neurotic anxiety reactions, and may be considered just as "irrational." Performance anxiety is, in fact, traditionally considered a form of anxiety hysteria (Hinsie and Campbell 1960).

Perhaps even more important is the relatively high incidence of interpersonal-performance anxiety in a large population of persons who are essentially "psychiatrically normal." Because of their essentially normal adjustment, students debilitated by performance anxiety do not pose the many complex problems encountered in patient populations. Therefore it is possible to obtain large enough samples of subjects with homogeneous problems to form comparable groups for careful, relatively direct investigation into conflicting methods of behavior modification. Furthermore, a public-speaking situation provides a prototypic stress situation for the elicitation of interpersonal-performance anxiety which permits the use of external criteria. Because courses in public speaking are required for a great many students, avoidance behavior is thwarted. As a result, the motivation to overcome these emotional reactions is much stronger than that found in laboratory analogies of psychotherapeutic studies. Aside from its obvious value to students of speech (Clevenger 1959) and college counselors (Marzolf 1962, Halio 1963), a study of performance anxiety manifested in public speaking should serve as a profitable starting point for the study of broader emotional problems.

Objectives

In accordance with the above considerations, the following comparative therapy study was designed with six specific objectives:

(1) To examine the relative efficacy and efficiency of procedures derived from "disease" and "learning" models in the treatment of anxiety—specifically, to compare traditional insight-oriented psychotherapy with modified systematic desensitization for the reduction of interpersonal-performance anxiety manifested in public speaking.

(2) To evaluate the contribution of nonspecific effects of individual treatment, such as expectation of relief, therapeutic relationship (attention, warmth, and interest of the therapist), suggestion, "faith," or general "placebo effects."

(3) To compare and evaluate the effects of individual treat-

ment with the effects of interviewing, testing, and traditional speech-course instruction.

(4) To determine the degree of anxiety reduction that results only from additional practice, personal contact, and expectation of future treatment.

(5) To demonstrate a feasible model for investigating outcome effects of behavior modification under "real-life" conditions, providing more rigorous controls and criteria than are now attainable in pure field studies.

(6) To add to the construct validation of promising measuring instruments.

METHOD

Ninety-six subjects, rated high on performance anxiety and motivated for treatment, were obtained from a population of 710 students enrolled in a public-speaking course (required for most undergraduates) at the University of Illinois. All students had completed a battery of personality and anxiety scales. Stress-condition measures were obtained on 74 subjects during a test speech, following which the subjects were assigned to one of five groups: three treatment groups (insight, desensitization, or attention-placebo), a "no-treatment" class control, and a "no-contact" control. After a time-limited treatment period, the relative efficacy of the various treatments in alleviating anxiety was then evaluated on the basis of measures obtained from the criterion test speech and from the follow-up battery of personality and anxiety scales.*

Instruments

Pretreatment Battery. The battery of scales administered to the speech-class population after the first classroom speech included: the Anxiety Differential (Husek and Alexander 1963); the IPAT Anxiety Scale Questionnaire (Cattell 1957); the Pittsburgh Social Extroversion-Introversion and Emotionality Scales, including the

* The entire population was also rated by the course instructors on the first, third, and sixth of six required classroom speeches, but the ratings are of no value to the present study because (a) only five of the 26 instructors consistently completed the ratings in the manner required, (b) at least seven of the instructors "discovered" or partially "discovered" the identity of participating subjects from their sections, thus invalidating the requirement of blind ratings, and (c) a number of instructors were unable to identify or discriminate anxiety, through lack of experience, halo, or other rating difficulties. Obtained course grades were also invalidated by the unknown effects of knowledge of participation.

MMPI L-scale (Bendig 1962); the Interpersonal Anxiety Scales ("Speech Before a Large Group," "Competitive Contest," "Job Interview," "Final Course Examination") from the S-R Inventory of Anxiousness (Endler, Hunt, and Rosenstein 1962); and a short form of the (PRCS) Personal Report of Confidence as a Speaker (Gilkenson 1942). The short form PRCS was constructed in order to satisfy time restrictions and improve the psychometric characteristics of the questionnaire. This form (see Appendix B) consists of the 30 most discriminating items (without exact mirror images) from Gilkenson's original 104; half of the 30 are keyed "true" and half "false" for experienced performance anxiety, yielding a single score. A Data Sheet requesting demographic information, time schedules, and motivation for treatment was also filled out by the students.

Follow-up Battery. The battery of scales administered on completion of the speech course was identical to the pretreatment battery; the Data Sheet, however, was revised to obtain from each treatment subject an evaluation of his own improvement and a rating of his therapist's likability and competence. The subjects were also given an opportunity to request additional treatment and obtain the results of the battery (see Appendix A).

Pre and Post Stress-Condition Measures. The measures of anxiety and physiological arousal taken immediately before each test speech were: the Anxiety Differential; pulse rate (the PR, taken by the investigator from the radial artery of the right arm in resting position, was counted for 30 seconds, timed by a stopwatch, recorded on a coded card to keep measures as blind as possible, and later converted to PR/minute by doubling); and the Palmar Sweat Index (PSI) by a photometric technique (Kuno 1956).*

During presentation of test speeches, each subject was scored on

---

* The PSI was obtained by a photometric process using commercial film and printer No. 6000 from Lab Line Instruments, Inc., Chicago. The solution was the one prescribed by Light (Mowrer 1953), and was prepared 3 days prior to use in both pretreatment and posttreatment tests. Prints were always taken from the middle finger of the left hand, with 30 seconds allowed for drying time before the finger was inserted into the printer. The film was pressed against the finger for 30 seconds with a constant pressure of 1 pound. Final PSI readings were then taken blindly from a Lab Line No. 6010 densitometer exactly 35 days following the time of printing. It should be noted that PSI measures on this equipment

the Timed Behavioral Checklist for Performance Anxiety (see Appendix B). This instrument, developed by the investigator, lists 20 observable manifestations of anxiety, the presence or absence of which is recorded by four trained observers during successive 30-second time periods of the first 4 minutes of a speech presentation.* Four advanced graduate students in clinical psychology served as paid observers. All four observers were trained together, for a six-hour period, in the detection and recording of behaviors with both live and video-taped speakers, so that all observers had a common definition of response. They were also instructed not to make judgments of "anxiety," but to indicate only the presence or absence of certain behaviors. The total score, derived by pooling the total incidence of behavioral manifestations over all four observers, thus served as an objective indicant of anxiety. The average inter-observer reliability exceeded .95 at completion of the training period.

The 20 behaviors recorded on the Behavioral Checklist are derived from those compiled by Clevenger and King (1961), and from observable clinical manifestations of anxiety.† The 20 behaviors are: Paces, Sways, Shuffles Feet, Knees Tremble, Extraneous Arm and Hand Movement, Arms Rigid, Hands Restrained, Hand Tremors, No Eye Contact, Face Muscles Tense (drawn, tics, grimaces), Face "Deadpan," Face Pale, Face Flushed, Moistens Lips, Swallows, Clears Throat, Breathes Heavily, Perspires, Voice Quivers, Speech Blocks or Stammers.

Therapist Ratings. Before working with subjects, each therapist

---

continue to increase in magnitude for approximately three weeks after printing, and then appear to stabilize. Additionally, interpretation of PSI raw scores should be disregarded, since absolute magnitude is a function not only of the degree of palmar sweat, but also of the distance between print swirls (*i.e.,* finger size). Change scores therefore appear to be the only meaningful data (Paul 1964a).

Appreciation is extended to Lab Line Instruments, Inc., Chicago, Dr. J. McV. Hunt, and the Veterans Administration Hospital, Danville, Ill., for the loan of PSI apparatus used in this investigation.

* A timing device, which signals "start," eight successive 30-second time periods, and then "stop," was constructed for use with this instrument by Merle Ridgley of Champaign, Illinois.

† Clevenger and King (1961) developed their checklist by reviewing the literature on the subject, and adding behaviors agreed upon by a group of experienced speech instructors.

completed self-ratings on a Therapist Orientation Sheet consisting of five-point scales in 24 areas (derived from Sundland and Barker 1962), and 20 specific therapeutic techniques (see Appendix C). At the completion of therapy, each therapist also rated each treatment subject on five-point scales for: likability, responsiveness to treatment, appropriateness of length and type of treatment, degree of reduction in performance anxiety, degree of improvement in other areas, indication of necessity for further treatment (prognosis), and therapist comfort in working with the client (see Appendix C).

Therapists

Five of the area's most highly regarded psychotherapists participated in the study, and were paid for participation.* Three were clinical psychologists and two were counseling psychologists; all held doctoral degrees and were highly experienced by usual standards. Two had completed 500 or more hours of personal analysis; two had completed 10 hours of personal psychotherapy; one had never undergone didactic treatment.

In addition to completing the scales on the Orientation Sheet, each therapist was asked to list the three authors who had been most influential in shaping his attitudes toward psychotherapy, and the "school" or "schools" of psychotherapy to which he felt most related (see Table 1). There was a relatively high degree of similarity in the specific orientations of the five therapists; their orientations (predominantly Neo-Freudian and Rogerian) also in-

* Members of our profession are to be congratulated for their willingness to submit their work to empirical evaluation. However, experience has shown, not only in this study but in others, that research in psychotherapy is not feasible unless therapists can be paid for the additional time. Anyone is justifiably reluctant to donate 50 or more hours to someone else's research when he is involved in research or practice of his own. Therefore therapy projects can suffer to the point of collapse from lack of rigor in administration of treatments and collection of data when "volunteer" time is involved.

Special acknowledgment is due to the therapists who participated in this study —Drs. Joseph Becker, Alice Jonietz, Merle Ohlsen, Fred Proff, and Donald Shannon—for spending extra time in rescheduling clients, completing forms, accepting and learning new procedures, and for agreeing to participate before definite knowledge of available funds was obtained.

TABLE 1

*Experience and General Orientation of the Five
Participating Psychotherapists*

Therapist	Most Influential Authors	Closest School Affiliation	Experience
1	Sullivan Fromm Dollard	Sullivanian Dollard & Miller	6 yrs.
2	Sullivan Freud Rogers	Sullivanian Neo-Freudian	16 yrs.
3	Bordin Pepinsky Rogers	Sullivanian Rogerian	18 yrs.
4	Freud Sullivan Rogers	Neo-Freudian	15 yrs.
5	Fromm-Reichman Szurek Rogers	Eclectic Sullivanian	12 yrs.

dicate that they are representative of the majority of similarly experienced psychotherapists who have been surveyed in other studies (Sundland and Barker 1962).

On the Orientation Sheet scales, the therapists differed by responding at opposite ends on only 8 of the 24 areas covered: Nos. 1 and 2, activity frequency and type; No. 9, source of goals; No. 12, client comfort and security; No. 19, nature of the learning process in therapy; Nos. 21 and 22, focus of therapeutically significant topics; and No. 24, curative aspect of the therapist. The therapists' responses to all 24 attitudinal orientations are shown on pages 16–17. These attitudinal factors demonstrate that if any bias existed prior to the administration of treatment, it was in the direction of the usual insight-oriented approach. However, all five therapists were selected not only because they had excellent reputations as insight therapists, but also because they possessed sufficient flexibility and open-mindedness to learn to use different, often conflicting, therapeutic theories and procedures.

Therapists' Responses on Therapist Orientation Sheet

1. Activity—frequency:

        Active.........|1..3..5|..2......|....4....|.........Passive
        (Talkative)   (Nontalkative)

2. Activity—type:

        Directive.........|1....4..|..2...5|...3....|.........Nondirective

3. Activity—structure:

        Informal.........|....3....|12..45|.........|........Formal

4. Relationship—tenor:

        Personal....3....|12..45|.........|.........|.........Impersonal
        (Involved)   (Detached)

5. Relationship—structure:

        Unstructured.........|.........|..2....5|1..34..|.........Structured

6. Relationship—atmosphere:

        Permissive....3....|..2..45|1........|.........|.........Nonpermissive

7. Relationship—therapist actions:

        Planned.........|.........|.........|12345|.........Spontaneous

8. Relationship—client dynamics:

        Nonconceptualized.........|.........|1........|..2345|.........Conceptualized

9. Goals—source:

        Therapist.........|..2......|1.....5|...34..|.........Client

10. Goals—formalization:

        Planned.........|....3....|12..45|.........|.........Unplanned
        (Formalized)   (Unformalized)

11. Therapist Comfort and Security:

        Always Secure.........|12345|.........|.........|.........Never Secure
        (Comfortable)   (Uncomfortable)

12. Client Comfort and Security:

        Never Secure.........|.........5|12......|...34..|.........Always Secure
        (Uncomfortable)   (Comfortable)

13. Client Personal Growth:

    Not Inherent.........|..........|12......|....345|..........Inherent

14. Therapeutic Gains—self-understanding (cognitive insight):

    Important..........|1..345|..2......|..........|..........Unimportant

15. Therapeutic Gains—emotional understanding (affective awareness):

    Unimportant..........|..........|..2......|1..3....|......45 Important

16. Therapeutic Gains—"symptom" reduction:

    Important..2......|1..34..|........5|..........|..........Unimportant

17. Therapeutic Gains—social adjustment:

    Unimportant..........|..........|..2..4..|1..3..5|..........Important

18. Therapeutic Gains—confidence in effecting change:

    Confident....34..|12....5|..........|..........|..........Unconfident

19. Learning Process in Therapy:

    Verbal-Conceptual..........|........5|12......|....34..|..........Nonverbal-
    Affective

20. Therapeutically Significant Topics:

    Client Centered..........|..2345|1.......|..........|..........Theory Centered

21. Therapeutically Significant Topics:

    Historical..........|........5|12..4..|....3....|..........Current

22. Therapeutically Significant Topics:

    Ego Functions..........|1......5|..2..4..|....3....|..........Superego, Id

23. Theory of Motivation:

    Unconscious..........|....345|12......|..........|..........Conscious

24. Curative Aspect of Therapist:

    Personality..........|1..34..|..2......|........5|..........Training

Treatments

Each subject assigned to an insight, desensitization, or attention-placebo group was treated individually. All therapists understood that the criterion of improvement was to be a reduction in performance anxiety. Since not only the efficacy, but also the efficiency, of psychotherapeutic approaches was considered important, treatments were limited to five contact hours (50-minute sessions) over a period of six weeks. Each of the five therapists administered each of the three treatments; therefore the amount of attention received and time involved was constant across groups, as were the potentially important effects of the therapist's prestige, personality, and physical attributes.

Insight-Oriented Psychotherapy (Group I). This treatment consisted of the traditional interview procedures used by the respective therapists in their daily work. With this approach, the therapist attempts to reduce anxiety by helping the client to gain "insight" into the bases and interrelationships of his problem. All therapists, even though they differed slightly in specific attitudes and approaches, felt that "insight" was an important therapeutic goal. In addition to his attitudinal orientations, each therapist indicated on five-point scales the extent to which he was accustomed to use specific techniques in insight-oriented treatment (Therapist Orientation Sheet, Appendix C). Table 2 presents the specific techniques rated and each therapist's placement on the scale. We may assume that the 20 specific techniques rated are inclusive because no therapist indicated additional techniques in the space provided. Tape recordings were made of each session to make sure that techniques other than the indicated insight-oriented interview procedures were not used. Three of the therapists gave a rating of 4 and two of 5 on a five-point scale of "confidence in effecting therapeutic change" with the insight-oriented approach.

Modified Systematic Desensitization (Group D). This treatment consisted of a slightly modified and formalized form of the treatment advanced by Wolpe (1958) and Lazarus and Rachman (1960). This technique of emotional re-education was specifically

TABLE 2

Frequency of Use of Specific Techniques by Each Therapist in Insight-Oriented Psychotherapy

Technique	Almost Always	50/50	Never
Reflection and Clarification of Feelings	....3....|1......5|..2..4..|..........|..........
Reflection and Clarification of Content	..........|1........|..23..5|.....4..|..........
Reflection and Clarification of Behavior	..........|1..345|..2......|..........|..........
Questioning of Feelings	........5|1....4..|..23....|..........|..........
Questioning of Content	..........|1......5|..23....|.....4..|..........
Questioning of Behavior	........5|1....4..|..23....|..........|..........
Interpretation of Feelings	..........|1..34..|..2....5|..........|..........
Interpretation of Content	..........|1........|..23..5|.....4..|..........
Interpretation of Behavior	..........|1..34..|..2....5|..........|..........
Suggestion (not hypnosis)	..........|..........|1........|..2345|..........
Reassurance	..........|..........|........5|12..4..|...3....
Information and Advice Giving	..........|..........|1........|..2345|..........
Attentive Listening	1..3..5|..2..4..|..........|..........|..........
Modeling Techniques (examples)	1........|....3....|......45|...2....|..........
Positive Attitude, Confidence	..........|12345|..........|..........|..........
Warmth and Understanding	....3....|12..45|..........|..........|..........
Reinforcement (approval-disapproval)	..........|..........|1..345|....2....|..........
Conditioning, Counterconditioning	..........|..........|..23..5|.....4..|..1........
Free Association	..........|........4..|123..5|..........|..........
Auxiliary Techniques	..........|..........|..........|1....45|..23....

NOTE: Therapists are numbered 1 through 5, as on the Therapist Orientation Sheet.

selected because it has been more widely used and can be more generally applied than other retraining procedures.

During the first treatment hour, a maximum of 10 minutes was spent exploring the history and current status of the subject's problem. Five to 10 minutes were spent explaining the rationale and course of treatment. Each subject was told that his emotional reactions were the result of previous experiences with persons and situations, and that these inappropriate emotional reactions could be unlearned by first determining the situations in which he becomes progressively more anxious, building a hierarchy from the least to the most anxious situations associated with giving a speech, and then repeatedly visualizing these situations while deeply relaxed. The subject was also told that relaxation was beneficial because the muscle systems of the body could not be both tense and relaxed at the same time, and that by proceeding gradually up the hierarchy, the previous anxiety-provoking situations would become associated with relaxation, thus desensitizing the anxiety.

The next 10 to 15 minutes of the first hour were spent in the construction of a spatial-temporal anxiety hierarchy (stimulus generalization gradient) made up of situations related to public performance, beginning with those that arouse very slight, controllable amounts of anxiety, and working up to those that cause extreme anxiety. The steps were carefully graded for minor increases in disturbance. A basic speech-anxiety hierarchy consisting of 12 items, from "reading about speeches alone in room, two weeks before a presentation" to "presenting a speech before the audience," was, with minor variations, suitable for most subjects (see Appendix D). The actual hierarchies contained 8 to 20 items, with some items from the basic hierarchy either dropped or subdivided to meet the needs of individual subjects. The subjects who completed their basic hierarchy in less than five sessions were given four additional items; these items were concerned with speech presentations to different and larger audiences.

During the last 20 to 30 minutes of the first session, the subject received training in progressive relaxation. This procedure, which is a much accelerated form of Jacobson's (1938), consists of alternately tensing and releasing gross-muscle groups, and learning to focus attention on these muscles, moving progressively through the body and extremities until a state of deep relaxation is achieved. The subjects were told to practice the relaxation procedure between sessions, twice a day for no longer than 15 minutes.

The second through fifth sessions were conducted in the following manner. The first 2 to 10 minutes were spent checking on the success of relaxation practice and correcting any problems with the procedure. (Practice in relaxation was usually terminated by the third hour.) Then, relaxation was induced (the process took 10 to 20 minutes, depending upon the subject), imagery was tested, and items from the anxiety hierarchy visualized according to formal rules of presentation (Appendix D), starting with the least disturbing items from the hierarchy and working up to the most disturbing. Two to 11 different items were presented in a single session; each item was presented 2 to 10 times for a period of 3 to 30 seconds. During the last few minutes of each session, following the successful presentation of an item, the subject was aroused and reactions to images discussed. The therapists were instructed to maintain a warm, interested, and helpful attitude as in any therapeutic relationship. Any questions were to be answered within a social-learning framework at a general level. Discussion of dynamics was not permitted. These last restrictions are not generally applied to systematic-desensitization procedures, but were considered necessary for this research.

Since the therapists were unfamiliar with this procedure, each underwent intensive training prior to work with subjects. Each therapist was given a manual that explicitly stated all procedures to be followed, including the time to be spent at various activities, and the rationale to be given subjects (Appendix D). After the therapists had studied the manual, they participated in a one-hour group meeting, and spent a minimum of two hours in individual training, during which the investigator demonstrated the procedures. Tape recordings of this treatment, conducted by the investigator, were also provided for training purposes, and each therapist practiced on a number of persons prior to work with subjects.

A session-by-session check was maintained by tape recordings. The investigator met regularly with each therapist after listening to the recordings of each session and immediately corrected any deviations from procedure.

Before work with subjects, four therapists gave a rating of "5" and one a rating of "3" on a five-point scale of "confidence in effecting therapeutic change" with modified systematic desensitization.

Attention-Placebo (Group AP). In this group, an attention-placebo procedure, administered by the same therapists, was used to determine the extent of improvement from nonspecific treatment effects, such as expectation of relief, therapeutic relationship (attention, warmth, and interest of the therapist), suggestion, and "faith." As with Group D, therapists were instructed to maintain a warm, interested, and helpful attitude.

During the first treatment hour, a maximum of 10 minutes was spent exploring the history and current status of the subject's problem, to help "break the ice" and establish rapport. Five to 10 minutes were then spent explaining the "rationale" and course of treatment. The "rationale" consisted of a brief statement that the subject's emotional reactions were a result of previous experiences with persons and situations, and were similar to reactions engendered by any stressful situation. The subject was also told that this anxiety was largely the result of a low tolerance for stress, and that it could be overcome if he were trained to work and think effectively under stress. This training involved the taking of a "fast-acting tranquilizer," and working, while under the influence of the "tranquilizer," at a task that was normally very stressful and engendered a great deal of anxiety.* The subject was told that the drug prevented the occurrence of anxiety: not only would he not experience anxiety during the task, but with repeated practice his mind and body would gradually develop a tolerance for stress, so that anxiety would no longer occur in stressful situations such as giving speeches, even without the "tranquilizer."

* Dr. Charles Young of the University Health Service graciously provided medical support for the use of a placebo.

The "very stressful task" was presented as one used in a government project for stress training of astronauts: it consisted of identifying "disaster signals" from a number of sonar signals presented over headsets from a recorded tape. The subject was told that the usual increase in anxiety experienced while listening to these tapes was due to the combination of noxious sounds and difficult discrimination. This particular task was chosen because of findings made during previous research (Paul, Eriksen, and Humphreys 1962) that this tape, which emitted signals of 800 to 2,000 kilocycles recorded from a variable oscillator, not only failed to increase anxiety, but often produced drowsiness after continued repetitions.

When the subject "understood" and accepted the rationale, the drug (a 2 gram capsule of sodium bicarbonate) was administered. After making sure the subject swallowed the capsule, the therapist left the room for 10 minutes to "allow the drug to take effect." When the therapist returned, he "checked the pupillary response" by passing a penlight twice across each pupil, murmured "mhm," recorded the subject's pulse, and announced "you're ready now." (Occasionally, for credibility, the therapist "rechecked" before announcing readiness.) The headset and volume were then adjusted for the "stress tape," and the remainder of the first session was taken up with the subject's listening to the tape and responding "target" each time a "disaster signal" was heard. While this was going on, the therapist sat attentively, observing and recording the number on the tape counter each time the subject signaled. Five minutes before the end of the period, the tape was stopped and the subject's "reactions" during the session discussed; at the same time, the therapist assured him that treatment was progressing well. The subject's "pupillary response" and pulse were again checked, and he was told that the drug had dissipated on termination of the session.

The second through the fifth sessions were taken up with answering any questions that were raised, in terms of the rationale presented (the period never exceeded 10 minutes), and following the same procedures prescribed for the first session. These procedures were found to be an excellent attention-placebo treatment

because during 35 to 45 minutes of each session, no verbal interaction could take place, thus preventing the subjects from intro-
ducing "therapeutically significant" materials or catharsis.

Each therapist underwent training similar to that described
above for modified systematic desensitization. A manual (Appendix E) giving explicit statements of all procedures to be followed
was also provided for this treatment, and a session-by-session check
was maintained by tape recordings, followed by weekly meetings of
the investigator with each therapist. Before working with subjects,
the therapists rated "confidence in effecting therapeutic change"
with this treatment as follows: two 5's, two 4's, and one 2.

No-Treatment Classroom Control (Group TC). The 29 subjects
assigned to the no-treatment control group continued in their respective classes, as did the subjects receiving individual treatment.
This control group cannot be regarded as a complete control for
"spontaneous remissions," since during the treatment period, a
maximum of two classroom speeches were required. In addition,
all students were required by their teachers to read a short chap-
ter entitled "Emotional Problems of the Speaker" from the course
text (Bryant and Wallace 1960) just before the treatment period.
The no-treatment group followed the same procedures, under the
same conditions, as the treatment groups, with the exception of
treatment itself. Therefore they received extra attention from the
investigator in terms of at least one telephone contact, a short interview, participation in two test speeches, and the promise of
treatment sometime in the future.

No-Contact Classroom Control (Group CC). The no-contact
control group consisted of 22 subjects who met selection criteria,
but who, because of the limitations of time scheduling, were *never
contacted* personally. Subjects in this group merely took the pre-
and follow-up battery with the entire class population, and continued in the speech course. Since the members of this group were
in fact unaware of their participation in a therapy study, a fractional replication is provided for assessment of possible improvement resulting from the individual attention and practice obtained
by the no-treatment control group.

Subjects

A total of 96 subjects (68 males, 28 females), ranging in age from 17 to 24 years with a median age of 19, participated in this study. All were undergraduates, representing all four college years, with the median falling at the sophomore level.

These subjects were selected from the population of 710 students enrolled in Public Speaking who had completed the Pretreatment Battery the week following their first classroom speech. The Pretreatment Battery included a cover letter which stated that the purpose of the study was to determine "which people benefit most" from various types of psychological procedures used to treat anxieties (Appendix A). The letter also stated that the study was supported by the government, guaranteed the participants that their responses and participation would be kept confidential, and described the amount of time involved in participation and evaluation. Approximately 54 per cent of the population expressed a desire for treatment; those who scored highest on the performance-anxiety scales (PRCS $\geq$ 16, SR-Speech $\geq$ 35) and low on the falsification scale (L-scale <7) were contacted individually by telephone. Any student who was not sufficiently concerned about performance anxiety, or hesitated to commit himself for the eight hours involved, was excluded from the study. Students who, prior to contact, had entered treatment elsewhere or dropped the speech course were also excluded.

Those students who met the above criteria were scheduled to appear for the Pretreatment Test Speech after they had completed their second classroom speech. Additional screening for motivation was provided by dropping those students who did not appear for the scheduled evaluation speech. Final screening of the subjects took place in an individual interview with the investigator; at this point those students who had received previous psychological treatment, and those who reported a reduction in anxiety during the required classroom speeches completed prior to the treatment period, were to have been dropped; however, no subjects needed to be excluded for these reasons. Seventy-four subjects (52 males, 22 females) were accepted after screening; the sample was then assigned to the three treatment groups and the no-treatment control. Twenty-two subjects (16 males, 6 females) who met all other criteria but who were never contacted, even by telephone, constituted the no-contact control group.

The subjects thus selected were "good bets" for psychotherapy (strong motivation, disturbing problems, relatively high intelligence, middle class, young, etc.). The subjects' degree of anxiety was strong to severe in most cases, and was reported to be of two-to-twenty-years duration. In addition to high performance-anxiety scores, the subjects reported many problems characteristic of anxiety, for example, nausea, mental confusion, "black-out," vertigo, tremors, excessive perspiration, accelerated pulse rate, rigidity, speech disturbances, tension, headache, insomnia, depression, avoidance behavior. Anxiety was seldom reported to be restricted to the speech situation, although it was usually more severe in that setting. In most cases anxiety was present in almost any social, interpersonal, or evaluative situation: competing in contests, answering roll-call, meeting strangers, taking examinations, making appointments and dates, bidding at auctions, and carrying on casual conversation.

Procedure

The basic plan of the study is presented in Table 3. Following administration of the Pretreatment Battery in the classroom, the subjects (except Group CC) were contacted individually, screened, and then scheduled for the Pretreatment Test Speech. Pretreatment Test Speeches were conducted in groups of six to 13, with the rest of the subjects, plus the four observers, serving as an audience for each presentation. No more than two subjects from the same class section were assigned to the same test group, so that each speaker's presentation was made before an unfamiliar audience of at least ten persons. All test speeches were conducted in the same classroom, which was just large enough to accommodate 25 people. The room was maintained at a constant temperature of approximately 72° F., and a relative humidity of 50 per cent.

For each test group, speaker order was randomly assigned and

TABLE 3

General Experimental Design and Procedure

Group	Pretreatment Battery	Pretreatment Test Speech	Interview	Treatment	Posttreatment Test Speech	Follow-up Battery
D (N = 15)	Anx. Diff. PRCS Extroversion Emotionality IPAT Anxiety SR Inventory Data Sheet	Anx. Diff. PR PSI Checklist	Interview and Assignment to Treatment	Systematic Desensitization	Anx. Diff. PR PSI Checklist	Anx. Diff. PRCS Extroversion Emotionality IPAT Anxiety SR Inventory Self-Ratings
I (N = 15)				Insight Psychotherapy		
AP (N = 15)				Attention-Placebo		
TC (N = 29)				Classroom Only		
CC (N = 22)	Classroom Only					

written on the chalkboard; seating was arranged to follow the order of presentation. The investigator explained that the purpose of the meeting was to determine each subject's reactions in a speaking situation. The procedure was explained, and the four observers introduced as "clinical psychologists and speech people who will be helping us evaluate your reactions." To equalize possible order-effects of anticipation, each subject was asked to complete a standard speech-critique form on approximately one-third of the speakers, always arranged so that the subject was "busy" during the two presentations immediately preceding his own. Just before his own presentation, when the preceding speaker went to the front of the room, each subject went to the back of the room where the investigator obtained stress measures. Because each speaker was asked to conclude his speech at the end of four minutes (the end of the period was indicated by a light from the Checklist timer), stress measures were obtained at a standard time. Four minutes before presentation, the Anxiety Differential was administered; the PR was taken 1.5 minutes before presentation, and the PSI during the 30 seconds immediately preceding each speech. During each presentation, timed Checklist frequency counts were taken by the trained observers. All subjects were given appointment cards to meet the investigator for a short interview following the Pretreatment Test speeches.

These subjects were then rank-ordered on the basis of their pooled Checklist scores, and randomly distributed from stratified blocks to the four treatment and control groups. Five females and ten males were assigned to each treatment group, and seven females and twenty-two males to the no-treatment control group. The subjects were further redistributed among the groups to equalize representation of test group, class time, and course instructor, and to obtain homogeneity of Checklist mean and standard deviation. Within each treatment group, one female and two male subjects were randomly assigned to each of the five therapists.

The investigator then interviewed each of these subjects (time, 15 to 20 minutes) for screening and instructions. Common expectations concerning treatment were established by informing each subject that he fell among the top 10 to 15 per cent of the total class on performance-anxiety measures, and by presenting briefly, in a standard manner, the rationale and course of treatment to be undergone. Any subject whose expectations of treatment were much different from the one assigned, and who furthermore did not appear to accept the rationale, was reassigned to another treatment. This was necessary for only two subjects.

After checking schedules, each subject was given a slip of paper indicating the name of his therapist, and the date and time of the first meeting. In each case, the investigator made another attempt to establish common expectations and "placebo effects" by exclaiming, "Oh, you'll be seeing Dr. X. He's very good with problems of this sort. He's had a great deal of experience, and I think you'll find working with him to be not only quite helpful, but interesting as well." The subjects assigned to Group TC received the same information, except they were told that, unfortunately, one of the participating therapists was unable to work with clients during that semester. They were also told that because we did not want to ask anyone to work with a less competent therapist, we had "picked from a hat" the names of those students who would not be seen. The subjects in Group TC were assured that we would provide treatment the following semester for those who still wanted it; they were also told that it would still be necessary for them to return in a few weeks for another evaluation speech, since our measures would be meaningless without their participation.

The treatment subjects then worked individually with their respective therapists for five hours over a period of six weeks, meeting at the University Psychological Clinic, the Guidance and Counseling Center, or the Student Counseling Bureau. All treatments were carried on concurrently, and any appointments missed were rescheduled during the same week.

Within a week of treatment termination, all subjects in Groups I, D, AP, and TC were brought in for a Posttreatment Test Speech. In addition to the controls instituted during the Pretreatment Test Speech, care was taken to assign approximately the same speaking order as before, and to make sure that subjects from each group were equally represented in all posttreatment test groups. Additional possible sources of bias were reduced by using coded cards for recording of data, so that treatment condition was unknown to the investigator while has was taking anxiety measures.

To protect the anonymity of the subjects, the Follow-up Battery was administered to the entire course population six weeks following termination of treatment, during the last meeting of the class. A cover letter (Appendix A), re-emphasizing the confidential nature of the data and informing all students of the opportunity to receive interpretation of their scores, accompanied the Follow-up Battery to reduce the possibility of falsification.

RESULTS

An analysis of the change scores from pretreatment to posttreatment stress-condition measures provides the most stringent test of treatment effects. Not only are the measures involved more objective, but they were taken in a situation in which the target behaviors (cognitive, physiological, and motoric) were most likely to occur. Furthermore the great majority of subjects reported the Test Speeches to be even more stressful than others because they were given before an unfamiliar audience and evaluated by psychologists. Evidence of the stressful nature of this experience was further indicated by the refusal of two female and five male subjects from Group TC to appear for the Posttreatment Test Speech, even after several inducements were offered, including payment for their time. Of these subjects, four plainly stated that the speech was so "upsetting" that they would not appear again under any circumstances, and furthermore that they would never again go before a group after completion of the required speech course; one subject was rescheduled twice, and could not be reached after failing to appear the second time; another subject, after missing two appointments, claimed to be "too busy"; and one subject dropped the course during the treatment period because of extreme anxiety.

Before proceeding to results, the reliability of the Timed Behavioral Checklist needs to be documented, since this instrument had not been used before. The reliability of total score over observers, as calculated by analysis of variance (alpha), exceeded .93 for the Pretreatment Test Speech ($N = 74$), and .96 for the Posttreatment Test Speech ($N = 67$). This instrument proved to be not only objective but also very reliable when highly trained observers are used.

Stress-Condition Measures: Test Speeches

Each of the stress-condition measures was subjected to a modified three-way analysis of variance (treatments, pre-post, subjects) on the scores of the remaining 67 subjects who completed both test speeches. The summary of these analyses is given in Table 4. The means and standard deviations for both pretreatment and posttreatment conditions are presented in Table 5.

These analyses indicate highly significant pre-post changes on all measures except PR, and, more importantly, a significant treatment-by-pre-post interaction, indicating differential changes between groups. The treatment-by-prepost interaction for PR approaches significance ($p < .10$). Inspection of Table 5 reveals that there was little change for Group TC on any measure. Since these analyses do not include the seven controls who failed to complete the Posttreatment Test Speech and may therefore be assumed to have remained at the same, or an increased, level of anxiety, differences between treatment and control groups are likely to be underestimates.

Since pretreatment to posttreatment changes between groups were the major interest of this study, a finer analysis was carried out on change scores for each measure: two-sided tests of significance were used to determine the significance of differences in pre-post changes between groups. Figure 1 graphically presents the mean reduction in observable manifestations of anxiety, in cognitive experience of anxiety, and in physiological arousal for each group, computed by subtracting pretreatment from posttreatment scores for each subject. In addition, a physiological composite was computed by pooling standardized change scores from PR and PSI. The results of the *t* tests of the significance of differences in pre-post change scores between groups (Figure 1) are presented in Table 6.

All three treatment groups improved significantly over the no-treatment control on observable behavior, from the Behavioral Checklist, and on the immediate cognitive experience of anxiety as reported on the Anxiety Differential. The desensitization group was the only group to achieve a significant reduction in measures

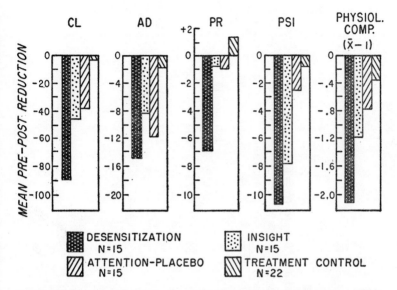

Figure 1. Mean reduction in observable manifestations of anxiety (CL), cognitive experience of anxiety (AD), and physiological arousal (PR, PSI, and standardized composite of PR and PSI) from pretreatment to posttreatment stress conditions.

of physiological arousal over the no-treatment control, although both the insight and the attention-placebo groups fell consistently in the same direction. Possibly the last two groups would have also achieved a significant reduction on the PSI and the Physiological Composite if the seven missing controls had been included. There was no apparent change in PR alone for these two groups.

Figure 1 reveals a remarkably consistent superiority of the systematic desensitization group on all measures; the insight and attention-placebo groups fluctuate, with first one and then the other achieving the second greatest reduction in anxiety. The reduction in overt behavioral anxiety manifestations for the desensitization group was significantly greater than that for either the insight or the attention-placebo groups. On the Anxiety Differential, the mean anxiety reduction for subjects treated by systematic desensitization was significantly greater (at the 5 per cent level)

TABLE 4
Analyses of Variance on Stress-Condition Measures (N = 67)

Source	df	Behavioral Checklist		Anx. Diff.		Pulse Rate		Palmar Sweat[a]	
		MS	F	MS	F	MS	F	MS	F
Treatment	3	11014.26	4.53[.01]	4.78	—	195.68	1.07	113.36	—
(a) error	63	2432.30		194.75		183.59		169.55	
Pre-Post	1	46865.94	52.37[.001]	1971.61	42.54[.001]	60.45	1.40	703.35	11.67[.001]
Treatment-by-Pre-Post	3	10209.46	11.41[.001]	264.26	5.70[.01]	97.61	2.27	170.16	2.82[.05]
(b) error	63	894.85		46.34		43.09		60.25	

NOTE: Superscript numbers are p values ($p < .05$, $p < .01$, $p < .001$).
[a] Only pre-post main effect and treatment-by-pre-post interaction are meaningful for PSI.

TABLE 5
Mean Pre-Post Anxiety Scores on Stress-Condition Measures

Treatment	Test Condition	Checklist		Anx. Diff.		Pulse Rate		Palmar Sweat[a]	
		Mean	SD	Mean	SD	Mean	SD	Mean	SD
Desensitization	Pre	212.1	47.91	80.2	9.22	92.7	9.65	23.1	8.33
	Post	126.9	27.23	66.4	8.16	86.1	8.72	13.1	8.42
Insight	Pre	211.6	41.50	77.0	10.11	84.7	10.48	21.1	7.26
	Post	169.3	33.52	69.3	8.68	84.0	7.97	13.7	6.90
Attention-Placebo	Pre	210.9	34.29	78.4	11.67	89.6	10.76	18.3	9.49
	Post	175.1	35.83	67.6	9.82	88.7	9.31	16.0	9.93
No-Treatment Control	Pre	213.6	44.17	74.5	12.42	88.7	13.19	21.1	9.55
	Post	210.9	43.46	73.1	12.37	90.2	10.19	20.6	16.56

NOTE: N = 15 for each treatment group; for the no-treatment control, N = 22.
[a] Only pre-post change, and not the absolute level of PSI, should be interpreted (see note to page 12).

TABLE 6

Tests of Significance of Differences Between Pre-Post
Change Scores on Stress-Condition Measures

		I	AP	TC
Behavioral Checklist	D	$2.57^{.05}$	$3.64^{.01}$	$6.44^{.01}$
	I		—	$2.42^{.05}$
	AP			$2.55^{.05}$
Anxiety Differential	D	$2.17^{.05}$	—	$6.09^{.01}$
	I		—	$2.24^{.05}$
	AP			$2.27^{.05}$
Pulse Rate	D	1.90^{a}	2.02^{a}	$2.25^{.05}$
	I		—	—
	AP			—
Palmar Sweat	D	—	$2.61^{.05}$	$2.57^{.05}$
	I		1.59	1.77
	AP			—
Physiological Composite	D	1.88^{a}	$7.16^{.01}$	$3.70^{.05}$
	I		—	1.29
	AP			—

NOTE: Superscript numbers are p values. Table entries are t values, $t < 1$ not entered. $N = 15$ for each treatment group; for the no-treatment control, $N = 22$.

 [a] $p < .10$ (two-sided tests).

than that for subjects treated by insight, but it was not greater than that for subjects treated by attention-placebo. Additionally, the reduction in Physiological Composite of the desensitization group over the attention-placebo group was highly significant, but failed to reach the 5 per cent level with a two-sided test when compared with the insight group. On individual measures of physiological arousal, the PSI reduction of the desensitization group was found to be significantly greater than that of the attention-placebo group but not of the insight group, while the mean reduction in PR reached only the 10 per cent level of significance between subjects who received systematic desensitization and those who received either insight or attention-placebo treatments. Inspection of changes between groups on individual behaviors of the Checklist also revealed major reductions for the desensitization group in behaviors considered to have an autonomic referent, e.g., tremors (see Appendix F). The only outstanding improvement for insight-treated subjects over the other two treatment groups was more frequent eye contact; on the other Checklist behaviors there were few differences between the insight and attention-placebo groups. In fact, in *no* case, for *any* of the five stress-condition measures, were significant differences found between the mean anxiety reduction achieved by subjects who received insight-oriented psychotherapy and those who received attention-placebo treatment.

Since clinical workers are more often concerned with percentage improvement in individual cases than with parametric group differences, the stress-condition data were further evaluated on the basis of individually significant change scores to facilitate comparison with other outcome studies. An individual case was classified as "significantly improved" on the Checklist and Anxiety Differential if pre-post reduction in anxiety score was greater than 1.65 times the standard error of measurement for the instrument. A classification of "significantly improved" on physiological data was assigned to those cases in which the Physiological Composite equaled or exceeded a composite equal to a reduction of 2 PSI points and 4 beats per minute PR (double the maximum recording error for each measure).

Improvement rates presented for each measure in Table 7 again

TABLE 7

Percentage of Cases Significantly "Improved"
on Stress-Condition Measures

Treatment Group	N	Behavioral Checklist	Anxiety Differential	Physiological Composite
Desensitization	15	100%	100%	87%
Insight	15	60%	53%	53%
Attention-Placebo	15	73%	47%	47%
No-Treatment Control	22	32%	9%	36%
	(29)	(24%)	(7%)	(28%)
Chi Square ($df = 3$)	67	19.87[.001]	33.24[.001]	9.51[.05]

NOTE: Superscript numbers are *p* values. The first set of figures presented for no-treatment control excludes the seven controls who failed to appear, presumably because of the degree of anxiety experienced under stress conditions; the second set of figures includes them. The per cent "improved" for the no-treatment control group with N = 29 is, therefore, more representative; however, Chi Square Tests were computed only on subjects actually completing the Posttreatment Test Speech.

disclose significant differences between treatment groups not only in the cognitive aspects of anxiety (from self-report), but also in the objective, observable aspects of physiological and motoric behavior. Particularly striking is the finding of a significant reduction in the cognitive experience of anxiety and in observable behavior in *every* case treated by systematic desensitization; in addition, a reduction in the physiological index was recorded in the great majority of cases. The improvement rates for the attention-placebo group are equally impressive: the 40 per cent increase over the control group in self-report measures was not unexpected, but the relative increase of almost 50 per cent over the control group in observable behavior, resulting only from attention-placebo effects, was a finding far exceeding expectations.

By comparing the percentage of subjects "improved" under the attention-placebo treatment with those "improved" under insight-oriented psychotherapy and systematic desensitization, it is possible to estimate the percentage of additional subjects who benefited from either the achivement of "insight" or "emotional re-education," over and above the nonspecific effects of "undergoing treatment." These comparisons reveal an additional improvement of 53 per cent on cognitive, 27 per cent on behavioral, and 40 per cent on physiological indicants of anxiety, over improvement expected from attention-placebo effects for subjects receiving systematic desensitization. On the other hand, "insight" produced a gain of only 6 per cent (one subject) on cognitive and physiological aspects, and *less* observable behavioral effects (by 13 per cent) than attention-placebo.

For practicing therapists working with individual clients, overall improvement in all three behavioral areas would usually be considered more meaningful than specific anxiety reduction in physiological, cognitive, or motoric areas. Therefore, individual subjects were further classified into the traditional global improvement categories in the following manner: those subjects who demonstrated significant anxiety reduction in all three areas were classified "much improved"; those who achieved significant reduction in any two areas were classified "improved"; and those who met the criteria on only one measure were classified "slightly improved." Individual subjects who met the criteria on none of the measures were classified "unimproved." The summary of this breakdown of cases is presented in Table 8.

In Table 8 we can see that some degree of anxiety reduction was achieved in 45 per cent of those cases in which the only "treatment" consisted of the usual classroom procedure, participation in evaluation speeches of the study, and minimal contact with the investigator. It should be remembered, however, that the amount of reduction was slight (Figure 1). The improvement rate of the subjects who received attention-placebo treatment was 35 per cent higher than the improvement rate expected for subjects without treatment contact, while the subjects who received insight and desensitization treatments demonstrate, respectively, an additional 48 and 55 per cent minimal improvement over no-treatment controls. The insight group showed a slight gain over attention-placebo (13 per cent or two subjects) when all measures were combined. Those subjects who received systematic desensitization maintained the high improvement rate reported above.

Since few therapists or clients would be satisfied with a "slight" degree of improvement, it might be more practical to compare "therapeutic success" by using the traditional combination of "improved" and "much improved" categories (therapeutic success being defined as a significant reduction in at least two of the three areas). When cases are collapsed in this manner, both insight and attention-placebo success rates fall at 47 per cent, an increase of

TABLE 8

Percentage Breakdown of Cases in Traditional "Improvement"
Categories from Stress-Condition Data

Treatment	Unimproved	Slightly Improved	Improved	Much Improved
Desensitization			14%	86%
Insight	7%	47%	27%	20%
Attention-Placebo	20%	33%	47%	
Treatment Control	55%	28%	17%	

NOTE: N = 15 for each treatment group; for the no-treatment control, N = 29.

30 per cent over the untreated group, and systematic desensitization remains at 100 per cent therapeutic success.

Follow-up Battery: Performance-Anxiety Scales

Data from pre-post changes on the paper-and-pencil battery are
based on a total number of 92. All subjects in the three treated
groups completed the follow-up battery. Only 28 no-treatment controls completed the follow-up battery because one subject had
dropped the course. Of the 22 subjects in the no-contact control
group, two had dropped the course and one entered treatment
elsewhere, leaving 19 subjects with follow-up scores.

Two scales of the battery (the PRCS and SR-speech) focus specifically on performance anxiety in the speech situation. The PRCS
is the most meaningful scale for assessment of specific target effects
of treatment, since the final speech of the course, which was completed after termination of treatment and which was the major determinant of the course grade, was taken as a reference. While the
PRCS is a report of "experienced" anxiety, the SR-speech scale
reports anxiety of an expected or "hypothetical" sort since the
subjects' reports are based upon a situation they had not actually
experienced.

The summaries of analyses of variance performed on PRCS and
SR-speech scores from pretreatment to follow-up are presented in
Table 9; means are presented in Table 10. Highly significant main

TABLE 9

*Analyses of Variance on Self-Report of "Experienced" Performance
Anxiety (PRCS), and "Hypothetical" Performance Anxiety
(SR-speech) from Pretreatment to Follow-up*

Source	df	PRCS		SR-speech	
		MS	F	MS	F
Treatment	4	122.68	$4.68^{.001}$	76.22	1.18
(a) error	87	26.23		64.54	
Pre-Post	1	1734.92	$146.69^{.001}$	724.05	$20.62^{.001}$
Treatment-by-					
Pre-Post	4	152.17	$12.87^{.001}$	146.78	$4.18^{.01}$
(b) error	87	11.83		35.11	

NOTE: Superscript numbers are *p* values.

TABLE 10

*Mean Self-Report Scores for "Experienced" Performance Anxiety (PRCS)
and "Hypothetical" Performance Anxiety (SR-speech)
before Treatment and at Follow-up*

Treatment	Condition	PRCS		SR-speech	
		Mean	SD	Mean	SD
Desensitization	Pre	21.9	3.50	46.4	6.89
	Follow-up	9.7	4.06	37.5	6.84
Insight	Pre	21.0	2.16	47.8	3.78
	Follow-up	14.8	5.34	43.3	6.36
Attention-	Pre	19.3	2.24	46.6	6.31
Placebo	Follow-up	10.4	4.35	38.5	5.26
No-Treatment	Pre	21.6	3.03	45.9	6.87
Control	Follow-up	16.6	5.56	43.7	8.99
No-Contact	Pre	19.1	3.92	44.0	6.35
Control	Follow-up	18.2	5.66	44.9	7.37

NOTE: $N = 15$ for each treatment group; $N = 28$ for the no-treatment control, and $N = 19$ for the no-contact control.

effects for pre-post change were found on both scales; and a significant treatment main effect was also obtained for the PRCS. More importantly, the treatment-by-pre-post interaction was found to be highly significant on both scales, indicating that there were differential changes between groups at follow-up.

The pretreatment means between groups were quite homogeneous, even though only the Checklist scores of the four contact groups (I, D, AP, and TC) were matched, and three of the higher scoring no-contact controls were excluded. The mean reduction in reports of experienced performance anxiety and hypothetical performance anxiety for each group is presented graphically in Figure 2. Results of two-sided tests of significance of differences between change scores are presented in Table 11. With the exception of a greater improvement for the no-treatment control group, the relative anxiety reduction found from reports at follow-up was quite consistent with that obtained for the cognitive experience of anxiety taken under stress conditions at termination of the treatment period (compare the PRCS reductions in Figure 2 with reductions for the Anxiety Differential in Figure 1).

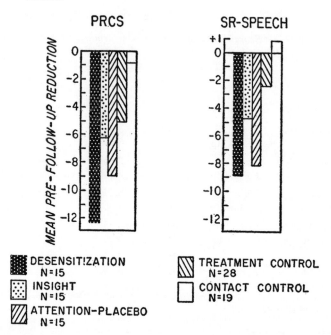

Figure 2. Mean reduction in self-report of experienced performance anxiety (PRCS) and "hypothetical" performance anxiety (SR-speech) from pretreatment to follow-up.

The significance tests presented in Table 11 show that the desensitization group's reduction in experienced performance anxiety was significantly greater than all the other groups'. The anxiety reduction for the group that received attention-placebo treatment was significantly greater than that for both control groups, but not the insight group. The differences between the insight and the no-treatment control groups did not reach the 5 per cent level of significance, although both were significantly different from the no-contact controls. It seems the extra practice and individual attention given to the no-treatment controls did produce a significant reduction in reported anxiety.

An analysis of hypothetical performance anxiety revealed no essential difference between the desensitization and attention-placebo groups, although both achieved significantly greater reduc-

TABLE 11

Tests of Significance of Differences between Pretreatment to Follow-up Change Scores from Reports of "Experienced" Performance Anxiety (PRCS), and "Hypothetical" Performance Anxiety (SR-speech)

		I	AP	TC	CC
PRCS	D	$3.66^{.01}$	$2.33^{.05}$	$4.69^{.01}$	$6.96^{.01}$
	I		1.61	—	$2.90^{.01}$
	AP			$2.53^{.05}$	$4.81^{.01}$
	TC				$2.56^{.05}$
SR-speech	D	1.83^{a}	—	$2.64^{.05}$	$3.30^{.01}$
	I		1.48	—	1.86^{a}
	AP			$2.31^{.05}$	$3.02^{.01}$
	TC				1.09

NOTE: Superscript numbers are p values. Table entries are t values, $t < 1$ not entered. $N = 15$ for each treatment group; $N = 28$ for the no-treatment control, and $N = 19$ for the no-contact control.

[a] $p < .10$ (two-sided tests).

tion scores than either control group. The SR-speech scale did not reveal significant differences between any of the three treatment groups, or between the insight group and either control. However, the differences between desensitization and insight, and between insight and no-contact control, approach the 5 per cent level, and are consistent with the direction of the other results. The differences between the two control groups, while in the same direction as the PRCS changes, failed to reach significance on the SR-speech scale. It should be remembered, however, that comparisons with no-contact controls, and to a lesser extent with no-treatment controls, may be underestimates because of the differential loss of highly anxious subjects.

The other three scales of the S-R Inventory of Anxiousness report on performance anxiety in three different interpersonal-evaluative situations, none of which were the specific focus of treatment. Analyses of variance performed on each of these scales are presented in Table 12. No single treatment or pre-post main effect was found to be significant at the 5 per cent level, although the pre-post main effect for SR-interview approached significance. The lack of a significant treatment main effect indicates that the group means, presented in Table 13, did not differ significantly. Al-

TABLE 12

*Analyses of Variance on Additional Interpersonal-Evaluative
Scales of the S-R Inventory of Anxiousness*

Source	df	Contest		Interview		Examination	
		MS	F	MS	F	MS	F
Treatment	4	122.87	—	220.34	1.32	193.67	1.05
(a) error	87	134.91		166.66		185.20	
Pre-Post	1	.44	—	135.67	3.42[a]	.78	—
Treatment-by-							
Pre-Post	4	61.82	1.42	59.41	1.50	101.22	1.87
(b) error	87	43.63		39.65		54.22	

[a] $p < .10$; no F significant at $p < .05$.

though the treatment-by-pre-post interaction also failed to reach the 5 per cent level, the relative order of anxiety reduction reported for the contest, interview, and examination situations was quite consistent with the results for the SR-speech scale. The coefficient of concordance over these three scales was highly significant ($W = .89$, $p < .01$); desensitization and attention-placebo generally reported greatest reduction, with insight, no-treatment control, and no-contact control following respectively. Both control groups actually increased their anxiety scores on these three scales.

Follow-up Battery: Personality and Anxiety Scales

Although none of the other personality or anxiety scales in the test battery were concerned with the specific target effects of the short-term treatment, they, like the scales from the S-R Inventory of Anxiousness, were included to aid in identifying the sample and to check on the generalization effects of treatment, or conversely, "symptom substitution." The four remaining scales are: the Pittsburgh Social Extroversion-Introversion Scale; the Pittsburgh Emotionality Scale; the IPAT Anxiety Scale; and the Anxiety Differential (pretreatment to follow-up). Summaries of analyses of variance on each of these measures are presented in Table 15. Neither treatment main effects, nor pre-post main effects, nor treatment-

TABLE 13

Pretreatment and Follow-up Mean Scores on the Additional Interpersonal-Evaluative Scales of the S-R Inventory of Anxiousness

Treatment	Condition	Contest		Interview		Examination	
		Mean	SD	Mean	SD	Mean	SD
Desensitization	Pre	36.2	7.39	42.7	10.23	46.4	9.46
	Follow-up	36.2	6.78	37.3	7.96	42.4	10.07
Insight	Pre	40.5	8.15	35.3	9.92	42.3	9.64
	Follow-up	38.3	10.96	33.7	11.20	42.3	12.19
Attention-Placebo	Pre	38.3	10.32	35.7	7.70	40.7	9.11
	Follow-up	34.5	9.29	32.1	6.72	36.4	11.52
No-Treatment Control	Pre	33.4	9.15	34.1	10.06	38.9	12.02
	Follow-up	35.4	10.31	35.2	10.22	40.7	11.58
No-Contact Control	Pre	35.2	11.02	38.3	11.82	41.3	8.37
	Follow-up	37.4	6.07	36.8	10.48	44.6	10.20

NOTE: N = 15 for each treatment group; N = 28 for the no-treatment control, and N = 19 for the no-contact control.

Table 14
Pretreatment and Follow-up Mean Scores on Pittsburgh Social Extroversion-Introversion (SEI), Emotionality (E), General Anxiety (IPAT), and Immediate Anxiety (AD)

Treatment	Condition	SEI		E		IPAT		AD	
		Mean	SD	Mean	SD	Mean	SD	Mean	SD
Desensitization	Pre	14.2	6.79	20.2	5.52	41.1	9.81	67.4	11.78
	Follow-up	18.1	7.60	18.9	5.70	38.0	10.02	64.9	8.83
Insight	Pre	16.7	5.70	17.3	5.76	33.9	9.39	64.1	11.12
	Follow-up	19.3	4.16	17.3	6.57	34.3	10.33	66.6	10.38
Attention-Placebo	Pre	13.7	7.74	17.3	6.25	35.1	9.20	63.7	13.33
	Follow-up	17.3	7.19	16.1	6.97	30.2	11.10	59.5	12.25
No-Treatment Control	Pre	16.3	6.60	17.8	6.08	35.6	11.37	63.8	11.49
	Follow-up	19.7	7.21	16.2	6.37	33.1	10.75	65.1	13.95
No-Contact Control	Pre	17.6	5.91	20.8	5.43	40.8	12.18	66.6	11.20
	Follow-up	18.3	6.46	21.7	6.65	43.6	11.60	67.9	8.38

NOTE: N = 15 for each treatment group; N = 28 for the no-treatment control, and N = 19 for the no-contact control.

TABLE 15

Analyses of Variance on Pittsburgh Social Extroversion-Introversion (SEI), Emotionality (E), General Anxiety (IPAT), and Anxiety Differential (AD) from Pretreatment to Follow-up

Source	df	SEI		E		IPAT		AD	
		MS	F	MS	F	MS	F	MS	F
Treatment	4	49.37	—	143.87	2.06	599.50	2.98[.05]	151.16	—
(a) error	87	85.26		69.75		201.08		186.42	
Pre-Post	1	361.76	45.28[.001]	22.26	2.14	93.27	2.18	.02	—
Treatment-by-Pre-Post	4	15.77	1.97	11.32	1.09	794.27	18.53[.001]	65.37	—
(b) error	87	7.99		10.40		42.87		95.17	

NOTE: Superscript numbers are *p* values.

by-pre-post interactions were significant on the Anxiety Differential or on Emotionality, indicating that pretreatment measures (Table 14) did not differ significantly for these scales, and that treatments produced no significant differential effects. No significant treatment main effect or overall treatment-by-pre-post interaction was found for extroversion-introversion; however, there was a highly significant pre-post main effect. Inspection of the pretreatment and follow-up means for extroversion-introversion in Table 14 reveals a relatively large shift of scores in the direction of increased extroversion for all four "contact groups," (Groups D, I, AP, and TC), with a slight shift in the same direction for the no-contact control. Although the overall treatment-by-pre-post interaction was not significant, the greater increase in extroversion scores for the combined contact groups over the no-contact controls was highly significant ($t = 2.69$, $p < .01$).

Of these four, the only scale attaining a significant treatment main effect or treatment-by-pre-post interaction was the IPAT Anxiety Scale.* The three treatments and the pretreatment and follow-up scores from the IPAT Anxiety Scale were analyzed by two-sided tests of significance on change scores between groups. These analyses revealed only two significant differences between groups. By comparing the pretreatment and follow-up means from Table 14, we can see that the desensitization group obtained a significantly greater reduction in general anxiety score than the no-contact control group ($t = 2.10$, $p < .05$), as did the attention-placebo group ($t = 2.06$, $p < .05$). No other comparisons between groups approached the 5 per cent level of significance.

Self and Therapist Ratings for Treatment Subjects

Ratings by subjects undergoing formal treatment ($N = 45$) were obtained at follow-up as a part of the Follow-up Battery;

---

* Although this instrument provides separate part-scores for "covert anxiety" and "manifest anxiety," as well as the total score for general anxiety, the data presented are only for the combined total score, since the part-scores were highly correlated, and no differences were found to exist between them on separate analyses.

therapist ratings for each subject were obtained within a week of treatment termination (see Appendix C).

Our first concern is the subjects' self-ratings of improvement—both specific improvement in reduction of performance anxiety and general improvement in other areas. Three-by-five factorial (treatment-by-therapist) analyses of variance performed on each of these self-ratings are presented in Table 16. In no instance were significant differential effects found for either therapists or treatments. Inspection of the mean self-ratings of improvement (Table 17) reveals that all three treatment groups obtained mean ratings of much improved for specific reduction of performance anxiety, and somewhat–much improved in other areas. In other words, all subjects stated that they had benefited from treatment, and the

TABLE 16

Analyses of Variance on Subjects' Ratings of Specific Improvement in Performance Anxiety and Improvement in Other Areas

Source	df	Specific Improvement		Other Improvement	
		MS	F	MS	F
Therapist	4	.700	1.13	1.633	2.49
Treatment	2	.489	—	.600	—
Therapist-by-Treatment	8	.517	—	1.100	1.68
Error	30	.622		.656	

NOTE: No *F* significant at *p* = .05.

TABLE 17

Mean Scores of Subjects' Self-Ratings of Improvement at Follow-up

Treatment	Specific Improvement		Other Improvement	
	Mean	SD	Mean	SD
Desensitization	2.9	.680	2.3	.699
Insight	2.9	.805	2.7	.997
Attention-Placebo	2.7	.789	2.5	.884

NOTE: N = 15 for each group. No significant differences between groups at *p* = .05.

TABLE 18

Analyses of Variance on Therapist Ratings of Specific Improvement in Performance Anxiety, Improvement in Other Areas, and Need for Additional Treatment (Prognosis)

Source	df	Improvement				Prognosis			
		Specific		Other		Specific		Other	
		MS	F	MS	F	MS	F	MS	F
Therapist	4	2.745	5.88[.01]	3.034	5.06[.01]	2.444	4.78[.01]	2.745	2.69[.05]
Treatment	2	2.600	5.57[.01]	7.223	12.04[.001]	2.956	5.79[.01]	2.156	2.11
Therapist-by-Treatment	8	.378	—	1.250	2.08	.678	1.33	.544	—
Error	30	.467		.600		.511		1.022	

NOTE: Superscript numbers are p values.

particular type of treatment had no significant effect on the stated degree of improvement—a sharp contrast to both the specific measures of anxiety reduction obtained under stress conditions, and the self-report scales of the Follow-up Battery.

Unlike the subject self-ratings, the therapist ratings of subjects for specific improvement in performance anxiety and general improvement in other areas varied in a highly significant way, according to treatment (see the analyses of variance summaries in Table 18). The therapists' prognosis ratings also differed significantly according to treatment for performance anxiety, but not for other areas. The significant therapist main effect for both improvement and prognosis ratings indicates that individual bias played a part in the therapists' tendencies to give high or low ratings. However, since the therapist-by-treatment interactions were not significant for any scale, and since each therapist made an equal number of ratings under each treatment, these biases do not alter interpretation of the significant treatment effects obtained. In addition, every subject was rated as improving to some extent.

Table 19 reveals significant mean differences in ratings of specific improvement between all three treatment groups: the systematic-desensitization group was rated most improved, with attention-placebo and insight following respectively. Here, the rating order is exactly the same as that obtained on the Anxiety Differential under stress conditions, and on the self-report measures (PRCS, SR-speech) at follow-up. In contrast, mean therapist ratings of improvement in other areas reveal a significantly higher rating for insight subjects than for desensitization and attention-placebo. This complete change in direction from the findings on the additional anxiety and personality scales of the Follow-up Battery suggests that either the therapists were basing their ratings of improvement in other areas on changes not assessed by the Follow-up Battery, or that their biases in favor of the insight treatment were selectively affecting their perceptions.

There is some suggestive evidence concerning these two possibilities in the answers given by the subjects at follow-up to the open-ended question: "Please indicate other situations or areas in

TABLE 19

Mean Therapist Ratings of Improvement and Prognosis

	Improvement				Prognosis			
	Specific		Other		Specific		Other	
Treatment	Mean	SD	Mean	SD	Mean	SD	Mean	SD
Desensitization	3.8^x	.542	2.4^x	1.083	1.6^{xy}	.611	2.3^x	1.011
Insight	3.0^x	.894	3.4^{xy}	.800	2.4^x	.952	3.1^x	1.062
Attention-Placebo	3.6^x	.879	2.1^y	.929	2.3^y	.869	2.9	.957

NOTE: $N = 15$ for each treatment group. Any two means within a column are significantly different ($p < .05$, Duncan's Multiple Range Test) if they share the same symbol (x or y). Ratings of prognosis were reversed, reading "Need for additional treatment"; therefore the *lower* the rating, the *better* the prognosis.

which these meetings have helped." Those who received desensitization answered by mentioning specific situations, such as talking at house meetings, dealing with people, taking exams, participating in class, meeting people, and sleeping soundly. Attention-placebo subjects also tended to respond with specific examples: dealing with people, speaking in other situations, taking exams, talking to people, meeting people, controlling temper, taking everything easier, and worrying less. On the other hand, insight subjects tended to give more abstract examples, such as understanding their emotional problem, understanding themselves better, gaining more self-control, forming new attitudes toward goals, acquiring new attitudes toward their personal life.

This disparity suggests that both the therapists and the insight-treated subjects had a conception of "other situations and areas" quite different from the one held by the subjects in the other treatment groups. Perhaps this difference can be attributed to the possibility that the insight subjects might have responded to what Whitehorn (1959) has called "preferred values, . . . the therapist's conception of what constitutes value in life," thus appearing more favorable in the eyes of the therapists.

Even though the insight-oriented approach was the one preferred by the therapists prior to treatment contact (Table 1), the mean difference in prognosis ratings after treatment (Table 19) shows that the desensitization group was rated significantly higher than either insight or attention-placebo for specific prognosis, and that desensitization was rated higher than insight for prognosis in other areas. Apparently the therapists felt not only that subjects treated by systematic desensitization had achieved greater reduction of performance anxiety, but also that they had received enough benefits to require little or no further treatment. Although almost all subjects were rated as needing some additional treatment in other areas, subjects in the desensitization group received the lowest such rating, suggesting that there was a certain amount of "pathological bias" that grew out of insight treatment, since the insight subjects were also rated as improving most in other areas. Because of the method of assignment to treatment groups, because of the nonsignificant mean differences for pretreatment measures, and because of the therapists' own ratings of subjects' responsiveness to treatment, these differences cannot very likely be attributed to individual differences among the subjects. Analysis of variance (Table 20) and differences between means (Table 21) of the latter rating did not approach significance.

Further data on therapists' posttreatment attitudes toward the different treatment procedures are available from their ratings of the appropriateness of the length of time and type of treatment for individual subjects. Analyses of variance on these two scales are

TABLE 20

Analyses of Variance on Therapist Ratings of Appropriateness of Length and Type of Treatment, and Subject Responsiveness ($N = 45$)

Source	df	Type		Length		Subject Responsiveness	
		MS	F	MS	F	MS	F
Therapist	4	1.022	1.35	3.189	10.25[.001]	.889	—
Treatment	2	13.267	17.55[.001]	3.889	12.51[.001]	.556	—
Therapist-by-Treatment	8	2.739	3.62[.01]	.722	2.32[.05]	.389	—
Error	30	.756		.311		1.156	

NOTE: Superscript numbers are *p* values.

TABLE 21

*Mean Therapist Ratings of Appropriateness of Length and Type
of Treatment and Subject Responsiveness*

Treatment	Type		Length		Subject Responsiveness	
	Mean	SD	Mean	SD	Mean	SD
Desensitization	4.0^x	1.033	3.1^x	.618	4.0	1.155
Insight	3.3^x	.998	2.1^{xy}	.957	4.0	.730
Attention-Placebo	2.1^x	1.087	2.8^y	.748	3.7	.943

NOTE: $N = 15$ for each treatment group. Any two means within a column are significantly different ($p < .05$, Duncan's Multiple Range Test) if they share the same symbol (x or y). Ratings of appropriateness for length of treatment are bipolar with > 3 indicating treatment longer than needed, and < 3 shorter than needed.

summarized in Table 20. A highly significant treatment effect was found for both type and length of treatment. Means presented in Table 21 demonstrate that the therapists felt that subjects assigned to desensitization received the most appropriate type of treatment; insight was next, with attention-placebo rated in the inappropriate direction. Mean ratings of appropriateness of length of treatment show that the therapists felt that the subjects in insight therapy needed a period of treatment longer than five sessions, but that those in desensitization or attention-placebo received the appropriate length of treatment.

In addition to significant treatment effects for these two scales, Table 20 also indicates a significant therapist effect for length of treatment ratings, and a significant therapist-by-treatment interaction for both length and type scales. These differences are graphically presented in Figure 3, where one may see that the significant interaction for type-ratings is primarily accounted for by the low ratings for attention-placebo by therapists 1, 3, and 4, and the low rating for insight by therapist 1. In ratings of appropriateness of length of treatment, Figure 3 shows that therapists 1, 2, and 5 rated the subjects in insight-oriented psychotherapy as requiring more than five sessions to overcome performance anxiety; for all other treatments (except those in attention-placebo for therapist 1), five sessions were considered to be adequate. The significant

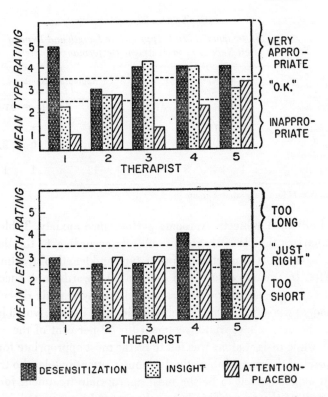

Figure 3. Mean therapist ratings of appropriateness of type of treatment and length of treatment for subjects within each treatment group.

therapist effect for length-ratings seems to be primarily a function of the difference between therapists 1 and 4.

Since all five therapists had confidence in their ability to effect improvement with the insight-oriented approach before actual treatment began, and since the subjects assigned to the various groups did not differ in any significant way, obtained differences would appear to reflect attitudinal and perceptual changes that took place during the treatment period. Further information about these changes was obtained from the therapists' answers to an open-ended question asking them to indicate the most appropriate type of treatment, and the appropriate number of sessions for help-

TABLE 22

Therapists' Statements of Most Appropriate Length and Type of Treatment Felt Necessary to Overcome Performance Anxiety

Treatment Received (5 sessions)	Appropriate Type of Treatment				Appropriate Number of Sessions				
	D	I	D + I	AP	3–4	5	6–9	10–20	25–50
Desensitization	13	1	1		4	9	1	1	
Insight	4	10	1		1	5	1	6	2
Attention- Placebo	4		5	6	1	12		1	1

NOTE: N = 15 for each treatment group.

ing individual subjects overcome performance anxiety. Table 22 summarizes the classification of subjects according to the therapists' statements of most appropriate type and length of treatment.

After treatment contact, and differential rewards from successful treatments, the therapists responded that systematic desensitization, or a *combination* of desensitization and insight, would have been the most appropriate treatment for 62 per cent of the cases seen, while insight alone was felt to be the most appropriate for 24 per cent of the cases. Interestingly enough, attention-placebo treatment alone was felt to be the most appropriate treatment for 13 per cent of the cases. This last finding may be accounted for by the fact that some therapists felt that the interpersonal relationship was the primary therapeutic factor in any treatment, and that the attention-placebo treatment did, in fact, constitute a genuine therapeutic relationship.

The emergence of a possible "pathological bias" in the insight-oriented procedure gains added support from the number of sessions the therapists felt were necessary for the subjects in each of the three treatment groups. Five or fewer sessions were considered adequate for 87 per cent of the subjects seen either in desensitization or in attention-placebo treatments, while only 40 per cent of the subjects seen in insight treatment were felt to have been able to overcome performance anxiety in five sessions. In fact, 53 per cent of the insight subjects were rated as needing from 10 to 50 sessions.

At treatment termination, the therapists rated themselves on the degree of comfort they experienced in working with individual subjects, and they rated each subject on degree of likability. Analyses of variance performed on both of these ratings are presented in Table 23. Significant therapist main effects were found for both scales, again reflecting individual rating biases. Therapist-by-treatment interactions were not significant for either scale; however, a highly significant treatment effect was obtained for ratings of therapist comfort. Mean ratings, presented in Table 24, show that the therapists felt significantly less comfortable working with the attention-placebo procedures than they did working with either of the other two. This finding is not unexpected, since the role the therapist had to play in the attention-placebo procedure was far removed from his usual role conceptions. However, the fact that ex-

TABLE 23

Analyses of Variance on Therapist Ratings of Subject Likability and Self-Comfort in Working with Subjects (N = 45)

		Subject Likability		Therapist Comfort	
Source	df	MS	F	MS	F
Therapist	4	2.245	$3.61^{.05}$	1.833	$2.95^{.05}$
Treatment	2	.956	1.54	5.067	$8.15^{.001}$
Therapist-by-Treatment	8	.428	—	1.233	1.98
Error	30	.622		.622	

NOTE: Superscript numbers are *p* values.

TABLE 24

Mean Therapist Ratings of Subject Likability and Self-Comfort

	Subject Likability		Therapist Comfort	
Treatment	Mean	SD	Mean	SD
Desensitization	3.9	.884	4.3^y	.854
Insight	4.3	.680	4.4^x	.800
Attention-Placebo	3.8	.909	3.3^{xy}	1.011

NOTE: N = 15 for each treatment group. Any two means within a column are significantly different ($p < .05$, Duncan's Multiple Range Test) if they share the same symbol (x or y).

ternal measures of improvement found that attention-placebo had effects that were at least as great as those of insight suggests that the relatively lower therapist comfort was not communicated to attention-placebo clients, or, if it was, had little effect.

Additional data on the above effects were obtained from the subjects' ratings of their therapists' competence and likability. Summaries of analyses of variance on these two scales, presented in Table 25, and means presented in Table 26, show no significant differences in ratings of therapist competence or likability according to treatment. However, a significant therapist main effect for likability, and significant therapist-by-treatment interactions for both likability and competence, were obtained. Mean ratings for each therapist by treatment group are graphically presented in

TABLE 25

Analyses of Variance on Subjects' Ratings of Therapist Competence and Likability (N = 45)

Source	df	Therapist Competence		Therapist Likability	
		MS	F	MS	F
Therapist	4	.356	1.88	.478	3.59[.05]
Treatment	2	.022	—	.422	3.17
Therapist-by-Treatment	8	.439	2.32[.05]	.311	2.34[.05]
Error	30	.189		.133	

NOTE: Superscript numbers are *p* values.

TABLE 26

Mean Subject Ratings of Therapist Competence and Likability

Treatment	Therapist Competence		Therapist Likability	
	Mean	SD	Mean	SD
Desensitization	2.7	.471	2.5	.499
Insight	2.7	.471	2.7	.442
Attention-Placebo	2.7	.512	2.9	.340

NOTE: N = 15 for each treatment group.

Figure 4. Therapist 5 was rated "very competent" and "very likable" by every one of his subjects in each of the three treatment groups, a possible reflection of the relatively greater stress this particular therapist placed upon the relationship factors in treatment. Therapist 4 was rated a close second for both likability and competence, receiving somewhat lower ratings from subjects treated by systematic desensitization. The other three therapists varied somewhat in obtained ratings; however, all therapists received mean ratings indicating that the subjects felt they were both competent and likable individuals.

In another section, the most meaningful analysis of possible effects on treatment outcome of all ratings reported above will be

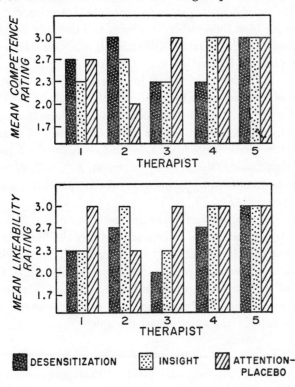

Figure 4. Subject ratings of therapist competence and likability in each treatment.

presented through intercorrelations. Here, however, overall effects may be evaluated by inspecting the possible therapist-by-treatment interactions within each measure of anxiety reduction. Accordingly, a modified four-way analysis of variance (therapist, treatment, pre-post, subjects) was carried out on the Timed Behavioral Checklist, and on the Anxiety Differential scores from the stress condition, and on the PRCS and SR-speech scales from pretreatment to follow-up. In addition, a two-way (therapist-by-treatment) analysis was performed on the standardized physiological composite (Pulse Rate and Palmar Sweat Index).

Analysis of variance on the Checklist yielded $F < 1$ for all three therapist interactions (therapist-by-treatment, therapist-by-pre-post, therapist-by-treatment-by-pre-post). Likewise, $F < 1$ was obtained for both therapist-by-treatment and therapist-by-pre-post interactions on the Anxiety Differential; the therapist-by-treatment-by-pre-post interaction was also nonsignificant ($F = 1.67$, $df = 8/30$). Furthermore, the F for therapist-by-treatment interaction was less than unity for the factorial analysis on the Physiological Composite. On follow-up measures of performance anxiety, all three therapist interactions for SR-speech yield $F < 1$, and the PRCS interactions, while higher, failed to achieve the 5 per cent level of significance (therapist-by-treatment, $F = 1.42$, $df = 8/30$; therapist-by-treatment-by-pre-post, $F = 2.24$, $df = 8/30$; and therapist-by-pre-post, $F < 1$).

In no instance, for any measure, were significant differences found between the overall effects achieved by the five therapists, or between the effects achieved by different therapists with the three different treatment procedures. Although attitudinal factors may be of academic interest, these findings suggest that they produce no overriding effects in short-term treatment conducted by relatively flexible and experienced therapists.

Construct Validity of "Improvement"

As Cartwright, Kirtner, and Fiske (1963) point out, a desirable conceptual variable in the realm of emotional disturbance and "recovery" should have a degree of "inherent meaningfulness" so that persons in different roles (or different measuring instruments) can agree or disagree systematically. In this study the key conceptual variable was a reduction of interpersonal-performance anxiety in public-speaking situations. Thus, for systematic agreement across different instruments, we would expect positive correlations between all change scores from each instrument purported to serve as an indicant of performance anxiety. Additionally, there should be a positive correlation between the subjects' ratings of specific improvement and the therapists' ratings of specific improvement, and a negative correlation between these two ratings and the change scores obtained by subtracting pretreatment from posttreatment measures of performance anxiety.

Table 27 presents the intercorrelations of change scores for the six separate measures used as indicants of performance anxiety under stress conditions and at follow-up. From this Table we can see that significant correlations, in the expected direction, were obtained between all self-report measures, and between observable behavior and both physiological data and self-report measures, but that no significant correlations were obtained between either physiological indicant and any self-report scale. The combination of PR and PSI into the Physiological Composite produced a positive correlation of .35 with change on the Behavioral Checklist, but still

TABLE 27

Intercorrelations of Change Scores on Each Measure of Performance Anxiety for the Total Contact Group (N = 67)

Measure	(2)	(3)	(4)	(5)	(6)
(1) Pulse Rate	$20.^{05}$	$29.^{01}$	08	08	−05
(2) Palmar Sweat		$25.^{05}$	14	05	16
(3) Behavioral Checklist			$43.^{01}$	$48.^{01}$	$32.^{01}$
(4) Stress Anx. Diff.				$38.^{01}$	$39.^{01}$
(5) PRCS					$62.^{01}$
(6) SR-speech					

NOTE: Superscript numbers are *p* values. Plus signs and decimals are omitted from the table. Change scores on measures (1) to (4) are from stress conditions; measures (5) and (6) are from pretreatment to follow-up.

failed to achieve a significant correlation with the three self-report scales. Inspection of prime correlations among the six measures of performance anxiety showed that the source of covariation in change scores resulted primarily from increased posttreatment relationships (see Appendix G). Several prime correlations were also significant even though the range was restricted by the homogeneous sample. Thus there appears to be a degree of construct validity to improvement in performance anxiety, even though "method factors" are still present.

Additional data, of both a convergent and discriminative sort, for the validity of improvement is seen in the correlations of both subjects' and therapists' ratings of improvement and prognosis with obtained anxiety reduction scores (see Table 28). Both therapist ratings (standardized to remove rater-bias) of specific improvement in performance anxiety, and therapist ratings of specific prognosis were significantly correlated, in the expected direction, with every indicant of reduction in performance anxiety, ex-

TABLE 28

Correlations of Subjects' Ratings of Improvement and (Standardized)
Therapist Ratings of Improvement and Prognosis with
Performance-Anxiety Change Scores (N = 45)

Rating	Change Score for Stress-Condition Measures			Change Score for Follow-up	
	Physiol. Composite	Behav. Check-list	Anxiety Differ-ential	PRCS	SR-Speech
Subject Rating					
Specific Improvement	20	$-50^{.01}$	$-33^{.05}$	$-46^{.01}$	-23
Other Improvement	20	-19	-12	-20	-01
Therapist Rating					
Specific Improvement	-19	$-44^{.01}$	$-41^{.01}$	$-43^{.01}$	$-35^{.01}$
Other Improvement	-10	21	04	22	05
Specific Prognosis	07	$51^{.01}$	$29^{.05}$	$55^{.01}$	$36^{.01}$
Other Prognosis	01	$45^{.01}$	$37^{.01}$	18	17

NOTE: Superscript numbers are *p* values. Plus signs and decimals are omitted from the table. Negative correlations between improvement ratings and change scores indicate agreement; positive correlations indicate agreement for prognosis ratings.

cept the physiological.* In the same manner, the subjects' ratings
of specific improvement were significantly correlated with the following indicants of anxiety reduction: observable behavior under
stress conditions (Checklist); cognitively experienced anxiety under stress conditions (Anxiety Differential); and self-report of
experienced anxiety at follow-up (PRCS). Self-ratings were not
significantly related to physiological data, or to reported "hypothetical anxiety" reduction (SR-speech).

An examination of the prime correlations between the six anx-
iety-reduction ratings and both pretreatment and posttreatment
scores for the six measures of performance anxiety revealed that
the posttreatment scores were the major source of the relationship
with the reduction scores; not only were there many non-zero correlations between ratings and posttreatment scores, but they were
changed in sign from corresponding correlations with pretreatment scores (see Appendix G). Thus, except for the physiological
data, there is consistent evidence that convergent relationships
exist between the various instruments and persons involved in
assessing anxiety reduction. Some suggestive validational evidence
of a discriminative nature may also be seen in Table 28, where
correlations of both subject and therapist ratings of other improvement with indicants of specific anxiety reduction failed to reach
significance. Therapist ratings of prognosis in other areas correlated significantly with stress-condition measures, suggesting that
these ratings were partially influenced by the amount of anxiety
reduction that was observed in performance anxiety for individual subjects.

The final relationships to be tested for the construct validation
of improvement are those between the subjects' ratings of improvement and the therapists' ratings of improvement and prognosis.
Significant correlations in the expected direction were obtained
between subject ratings of specific improvement in reduction of
performance anxiety and therapist ratings of specific improve-

---

* Each therapist also indicated the degree of confidence placed in ratings of
improvement; however, since all therapists were highly confident of their ratings,
they are combined for analysis.

TABLE 29

*Intercorrelations of Subject Ratings of Improvement and
(Standardized) Therapist Ratings of Improvement
and Prognosis (N = 45)*

Rating	Subject (2)	Therapist (1)	Therapist (2)	Therapist (3)	Therapist (4)
Subject Rating					
(1) Specific Improvement	$60^{.01}$	$37^{.01}$	-03	$-40^{.01}$	$-28^{.05}$
(2) Other Improvement		23	01	$-26^{.05}$	-19
Therapist Rating					
(1) Specific Improvement			-08	$-59^{.01}$	$-42^{.01}$
(2) Other Improvement				02	17
(3) Specific Prognosis					$56^{.01}$
(4) Other Prognosis					

NOTE: Superscript numbers are *p* values. Plus signs and decimals are omitted from the table. Positive correlations between improvement ratings and between prognosis ratings indicate agreement; negative correlations between improvement and prognosis ratings indicate agreement.

ment and prognosis (Table 29). However, in contrast to the relationships existing between other indicants of improvement, including self-report scales, this data shows a predominance of "method factor" within both subject ratings of improvement and therapist ratings of prognosis. This finding supports Zax and Klein's (1960) argument that one should not use ratings by involved participants as the sole, or even the major, criterion in outcome research. In addition, therapist ratings of improvement in other areas did not relate to subject ratings of improvement or to therapist prognosis in other areas, supporting the interpretation offered earlier, that biases were probably affecting these ratings.

The intercorrelations of indicants of improvement, or reduction in performance anxiety, demonstrate quite consistent relations of about the order .40 between the different scales and persons in different roles—with the exception of physiological data, which were significantly related only to observable behavioral change. These results not only justify the conceptual variable in question, but also support the admonition of Cartwright *et al.* (1963) to avoid using a single criterion measure. As Zax and Klein have suggested, the most promising criterion measure does in fact appear to be external observable behaviors: the Timed Behavioral Checklist was the only instrument whose change scores consistently correlated most highly with all other indicants of anxiety reduction.

Prediction of Improvement

Although it was not a major interest of this study, the ability to predict which persons respond to treatment would be of considerable value both in future research and in clinical practice. Recent theoretical discussion has centered around the possibilities of differential responsiveness to treatment according to the personality dimensions of extroversion-introversion (Eysenck 1961c, Franks 1961, Hovland and Janis 1959), emotionality (Lazarus 1963, Hovland and Janis 1959), and general anxiety level (Frank 1961).

In order to investigate possible relationships between these personality dimensions and improvement, the pretreatment scores of the total contact group (N = 67) on the Pittsburgh Social Extroversion-Introversion Scale, the Pittsburgh Emotionality Scale, and IPAT Anxiety Scale were correlated first with the reduction scores derived from the three stress condition measures of performance anxiety (Anxiety Differential, Behavioral Checklist, and Physiological Composite), and then with the two specific performance-anxiety scales from the posttreatment test battery (PRCS, SR-speech). Subject and therapist ratings of specific and other improvement, therapist ratings of responsiveness to treatment, and therapist specific and other prognosis ratings were also correlated with scores of the three personality scales for treated subjects (N = 45).

The results of these correlational analyses were totally nonsignificant. Of the 36 coefficients computed, only one attained significance at the 5 per cent level, actually less than expected by chance. Assuming that responsiveness to specific types of treatment might have varied with these personality dimensions, a further analysis was carried out to compare the differences between correlations of each personality scale with each indicant of improvement for the separate treatment groups. Again results were totally negative; the 90 comparisons made by Z' tests yielded only two significant differences at the 5 per cent level. Thus, for the sample included in the present study, neither extroversion-introversion score, nor emotionality score, nor general anxiety score were able to predict responsiveness to treatment in general, or differential responsiveness to specific treatments.

It would be unwise, however, to make too many generalizations from these findings: not only are the numbers small for correlational analysis, but the sample is quite homogeneous. The participating subjects not only scored high on interpersonal-performance anxiety and motivation for treatment, and low on falsification, but also differed from the population in other respects. A comparison of the sample's pretreatment mean scores on the various personality and anxiety scales (Appendix I) with the corresponding mean scores for the class population (Appendix J) shows that the participating subjects were more introverted, more emotional, and more anxious than the rest of the population. Intercorrelations of scales based upon the total population (Appendix J) suggest these relationships to hold not only for the treated subjects, but for the rest of the population as well; that is, those individuals who received high scores on interpersonal-performance anxiety scales specific to the speech situation also tended to receive higher scores on the general anxiety scale, the emotionality scale, and the interpersonal-evaluative anxiety scales, and lower scores on extroversion. Therefore the individuals who sought treatment were likely to be the most responsive, but they were also so homogeneous with respect to major personality dimensions that the treatment received did, in fact, account for the major proportion of variance in anxiety reduction.

Attitudinal Relationships of Subjects and Therapists

Other writers have suggested that the attitudes of therapists and clients toward one another, and toward therapy, often affect the outcome of treatment. Although all therapists involved in this study were rated both likable and competent by their clients, a significant therapist-by-treatment interaction was obtained for both likability and competence ratings, and a significant therapist effect for likability. On the other hand, therapist ratings of client likability yielded no significant differences. Although each therapist rated himself as feeling comfortable with clients in all treatment conditions, the attention-placebo treatment produced significantly lower therapist-comfort ratings than either insight or desensitization. The amount of anxiety reduction achieved on any measure did not differ significantly either for therapists using all treatments, or for different therapists using different treatments.

A clearer picture of the possible effects of attitudes on outcome of treatment emerges from the correlation of subject ratings of therapist competence and likability with performance-anxiety reduction scores, and the correlation of therapist ratings of subject likability, therapist comfort and confidence, with the same anxiety reduction scores (see Table 30). No significant correlations were found between the therapists' likability ratings and any indicant of anxiety reduction, or between subjects' likability ratings and

TABLE 30

Correlations of Attitudinal Ratings by Treatment Subjects and Therapists with Performance-Anxiety Change Scores (N = 45)

| | Change Score | | | | |
| | Stress Condition Measures | | | Follow-up | |
Rating	Physiol. Composite	Behavioral Check-list	Anxiety Differ-ential	PRCS	SR-Speech
Subject Rating					
Therapist Competence	09	−10	−06	−39.01	−19
Therapist Likability	−03	00	01	−23	−20
Therapist Rating					
Subject Likability	−21	−12	06	−15	−10
Therapist Comfort	−29.05	−43.01	−11	−12	−20
Pretreatment Confidence	−19	−12	21	04	03

NOTE: Superscript numbers are *p* values. Plus signs and decimals are omitted from the table. Negative correlations between any rating and change score indicate a positive relationship with anxiety reduction.

any indicant of anxiety reduction. Table 30 also shows that the therapists' pretreatment ratings of confidence in effecting change with a particular kind of treatment were not significantly related to reduction in performance anxiety. Prime correlations of these three ratings with performance-anxiety scores were also nonsignificant (Appendix H). Likability ratings and therapists' confidence ratings also failed to correlate significantly with subjects' self-ratings of improvement, or with therapists' ratings of specific improvement and prognosis. We may therefore conclude that differing degrees of likability or therapist confidence did not significantly influence the overall reduction of performance anxiety in this study.

Subject ratings of therapist competence were significantly related only to the PRCS reduction score. In addition, the follow-up PRCS score was the only significant prime correlation for that rating (Appendix H); this suggests that the subjects may have rated therapist competence to some extent on the degree of anxiety felt during the speech taken as a reference for that scale. No significant correlations were found between subject ratings of improvement and subject ratings of therapist competence, or between therapist ratings of improvement and prognosis and subject ratings of therapist competence.

In addition to the correlations shown in Table 30, therapist comfort was also significantly correlated with the subjects' ratings of specific improvement ($r = .33$, $p < .05$), the therapists' ratings of specific prognosis ($r = -.32$, $p < .05$), and the therapists' ratings of other improvement ($r = .48$, $p < .01$). The correlation of therapist comfort with therapist ratings of specific improvement approached significance ($r = .27$, $p < .10$). Since the attention-placebo group was the only group that received significantly lower therapist-comfort ratings, the above correlations were primarily the result of outcome differences among attention-placebo subjects. Of course it is unknown whether these subjects received less benefits because of their therapists' discomfort, or whether the therapists were relatively less comfortable because some subjects were less responsive to the attention-placebo procedure. Some suggestive evidence may be found in the correlation of therapist comfort ratings with therapist ratings of subject responsiveness ($r = .62, p < .01$) and with therapist ratings of appropriateness of treatment ($r = .49, p < .01$). Since therapists also varied in their acceptance of the attention-placebo procedure, it may very well be that their relatively greater discomfort was communicated to some subjects, who then became less responsive. The prime correlations between therapist comfort ratings and performance anxiety scores (Appendix H) show a shift from positive correlations on pretreatment measures to negative correlations on posttreatment measures, with the exception of PR. All of these results suggest that the attention-placebo procedure might have produced an even greater reduction in anxiety had conditions been optimal.

Although subject ratings of therapist likability and competence were essentially unrelated to outcome in the present study, the relationship of these ratings to similar ratings by therapists was felt to have some heuristic value. Therefore the subject ratings of therapist likability and competence were correlated with all therapist posttreatment ratings, and with therapist pretreatment ratings of confidence in effecting change. Subject ratings of therapist competence and likability were not significantly related to a single posttreatment rating by therapists. However, there was an interesting relationship between the subjects' ratings of their therapists and the therapists' ratings of confidence in effecting change: a significant negative correlation was found to exist between the therapists' ratings of confidence in effecting change and both the subjects' ratings of therapist competence ($r = -.32, p < .05$) and the subjects' ratings of therapist likability ($r = -.38, p < .05$). Although differences were slight for both therapist and subject ratings, the therapists who rated themselves most confident with a specific treatment before treatment contact were the ones rated least liked and least competent by clients. There is a simple explanation for this relationship: the therapists who had the most confidence in being able to effect change with the attention-placebo and desensitization procedures before treatment underestimated the complexity of the procedures, and thus required more supervision and "backtracking" during the treatment period. Those therapists who were less confident prior to treatment made a greater effort to learn and follow prescribed procedures from the beginning, and were thus more consistent during the treatment period.

One last source of possible influence on therapist ratings was investigated by correlating the therapists' rating of subject likability with pretreatment measures of extroversion, emotionality, and general anxiety, and by correlating appropriateness of length and type of treatment with the same pretreatment measures. As was the case with all other therapist ratings, no significant relationships were found between appropriateness of length or type of treatment and any of the three personality scales. With this evidence, the contention offered earlier that a degree of "pathological bias" resulted from the interaction taking place in the insight-oriented treatment gains added support. In contrast, therapist ratings of subject likability were found to be related to the subjects' extroversion ($r = .51$, $p < .01$), but not to their emotionality or general anxiety. Within this homogeneous sample of highly motivated, introverted, emotional, and anxious clients, therapists obviously preferred those who were more responsive, more extroverted, and whose values approached their own. However, in this study at least, these factors had little or no relationship to specific outcome effects.

DISCUSSION

The results of the present study clearly demonstrate the superiority of treatment based on a "learning" model (modified systematic desensitization) over treatment based on the traditional "disease" model (insight-oriented psychotherapy) in the alleviation of maladaptive anxiety. Desensitization therapy produced a consistently greater measurable reduction in the cognitive, physiological, and motoric aspects of stress-engendered anxiety, a reduction that was found to be maintained at the six-week follow-up period. Perhaps even more impressive is the fact that experienced psychotherapists, whose experience and biases were in the direction of the insight approach, rated subjects treated by systematic desensitization not only as improving more, but also as having a significantly better prognosis. In fact, after working with the procedure, the therapists began recommending systematic desensitization treatment, using the procedure with their own clients, and demonstrating it in conjunction with their training or consulting work.

The specificity of effects with systematic desensitization is greatly enhanced by comparison with the effects of attention-placebo. Desensitization was consistently superior to the attention-placebo treatment in all areas under stress conditions, on therapist ratings, and on self-report of experienced anxiety at follow-up. However, the differences between desensitization and attention-placebo were considerably smaller on self-report measures, and were actually nonexistent on the SR-speech scale of "expected" anxiety. This finding suggests that the primary results of the attention-placebo treatment were changes in attitudes and expectancies, rather than a direct modification of the emotional reactions associated with interpersonal-performance situations.

Therapists who have deviated somewhat from the traditional disease model of psychopathology have for years recognized changes in attitudes and expectancies as major goals of therapy, and as mediators of affective change by interview techniques (e.g., Rotter 1954, Kelley 1955, Frank 1961). It was not surprising, therefore, that no significant differences were found on any measure between the effects of insight-oriented psychotherapy and the effects of attention-placebo treatment. That is to say, if the results of traditional interview therapy are, for the most part, due to changes in attitudes and expectancies rather than to "uncovering the complex" or "passing repressions in review," any procedure that could mobilize these changes would also be expected to produce an equal degree of relief. Such was the case in the present study. In fact, on self-report measures the attention-placebo group consistently reported slightly greater (although not significantly different) anxiety reductions than the insight group.

The consistency of this finding suggests that the insight clients, because they were constantly confronted with the disturbing aspects of life-situations, and received relatively little reassurance, suggestion, information, and advice from their therapists, actually changed less in attitude and expectancy toward interpersonal-performance situations than did the attention-placebo group. On the other hand, the kind of statements the insight clients made about other areas of improvement (see p. 52) does indicate that additional attitudinal changes were brought about in the insight treatment. These changes appear to be, however, more in the direction of general attitudes and values held by the therapists, than in the direction of attitudes and expectancies related to interpersonal-performance situations. The latter interpretation is supported by previous studies by Heine (1953), Rosenthal (1955), and Palmore, Lennard, and Hendin (1959).

Many recent writers concerned with the lack of demonstrable effects of psychotherapy over no-treatment groups have argued that "spontaneous remission" does not occur, and that all studies to date are actually comparisons of "formal psychotherapy" with informal or "nonspecific psychotherapy" (Luborsky 1954, Rosenzweig 1954, Goldstein 1960, 1962, Frank 1961, Bergin 1963). Frank, Goldstein, and Bergin draw specific attention to the experimental studies in which a no-treatment control group undergoes interviewing and testing, and is often promised treatment sometime in the future. Writers such as Luborsky and Rosenzweig focus upon the fact that the base-rate improvement groups in Eysenck's (1952) review were seen by nonprofessional "psychotherapists" who provided reassurance, suggestion, and support, which are, to quote Rosenzweig, "techniques of psychotherapy."

In spite of the serious lack of comparability among the various populations reviewed by Eysenck (1952, 1961b), in spite of the near absence of meaningful criteria of improvement, and in spite of Eysenck's highly questionable practice of including in the "unimproved" category persons who had terminated treatment because of death or moving, the fact remains that these "studies" provide the only available data on the effects of formal psychotherapy and nonspecific psychotherapy as it exists in vivo. Comparing the combined improvement rates over all of Eysenck's studies, one finds about a 70 per cent minimal improvement rate for formal psychotherapy, and approximately the same figure for base-rate nonspecific psychotherapy. Although the sample of clients involved in the present study differs substantially from the usual study sample, and although the scope and criteria of outcome differ from those of in vivo reports, it is interesting that the percentage of "successful" cases (much improved and improved in all instances) runs at approximately 50 per cent for both the insight and attention-placebo groups of the present study, and for the combined reports of insight-oriented psychotherapy in the literature (Eysenck 1961b, Frank 1961, Colby 1964). In addition, reports of responsiveness to inactive placebos, while again not truly comparable, run from 30 to 70 per cent (Goldstein 1962).

Despite the acknowledged incomparability of all these studies, the relative consistency of results seems to be greater than chance: the gaining of insight from traditional eclectic or analytic psychotherapy does not appear to have been any more beneficial for neurotic individuals than the effects gained from the reassurance, suggestion, and support given by nonprofessional psychotherapists. In agreement with these findings, the present study, making use of the same criteria with the same amount of contact, and the same therapists, finds the same percentage of "successful" cases for both insight and attention-placebo treatments.

This study lends some support to Bergin's (1963) statement that no-treatment control groups are actually therapy groups. Comparison of changes from pretreatment to follow-up on the self-report scales revealed that the no-treatment controls, who were involved in all interview, testing, and contact procedures with the exception of formal psychotherapy, did report significantly less experienced anxiety on the PRCS, and a greater increase in extroversion, than the no-contact controls. Additionally, the no-treatment controls consistently reported more anxiety reduction on other scales than the no-contact controls, although none of the individual differences were statistically significant. When compared to the treatment groups at follow-up, the no-treatment controls were found to report about the same degree of reduction in performance anxiety reported by those subjects who underwent insight treatment, but significantly less anxiety reduction than either the desensitization or attention-placebo group. From the self-report measures it appears that the effects of undergoing interview and testing procedures, and the promise of future therapy, are as effective in bringing about favorable therapeutic change and anxiety reduction as insight-oriented psychotherapy.

This finding is in complete agreement with the findings of several studies reviewed by Bergin, in which no-treatment controls were included in the design. Perhaps the conclusion to be derived from all of the foregoing evidence is *not* that the comparison between treated and nontreated groups has little to do with effectiveness of therapy (Cartwright 1955), *nor* that psychotherapy is ineffective (Eysenck 1952), but rather that traditional insight-oriented psychotherapy is no more efficient in bringing about change than the nonspecific aspects of attention, interest, etc. Then one may legitimately ask, as Borgotta (1959) has, that if the same benefits can be obtained through testing and one interview, why should therapists continue to keep clients in treatment for months or even years? The fact that the desensitization and attention-placebo groups did demonstrate a significantly greater gain at follow-up than the no-treatment group provides further support for the superiority of non-insight procedures.

However, the effectiveness of the testing procedures in producing change may not be as great as suggested by the follow-up data; there may be as much "hello-goodbye effect" (Hathaway 1948) as "Hawthorne effect" (Roethlesberger 1941). This possibility arises from the relative differences in anxiety reduction found on the posttreatment stress-condition measures and on the follow-up data. In the stress condition, very slight reduction was achieved on any measure for the no-treatment controls, while the insight group demonstrated significantly greater anxiety reduction both in observable behavior and in self-report of the immediate cognitive experience of anxiety. Since the greatest amount of attention (telephone contact, pretreatment test speech, interview) was given prior to the posttreatment test speech, one would expect that the major portion of anxiety reduction for the no-treatment controls would have occurred by that time. Although it is possible that further improvement could be expected from the added attention, practice, and reassurance obtained from the posttreatment test speech, the relatively greater reduction obtained from self-report at follow-up for the no-treatment controls suggests that attitudinal factors may have been responsible. The no-treatment controls may have wanted to show that they could improve "in spite of" not being treated when they desired it. This again points out the difficulty in relying on self-report measures as the sole criteria of outcome.

In contrast to the literature on traditional insight-oriented psychotherapy, an increasing number of papers have begun to appear reporting very high improvement rates from treatments based upon a learning model of psychopathology. Indicating the current Zeitgeist, numerous review articles have appeared (Bandura 1961, Rachman 1963, Kalish 1965, Grossberg 1964, Goodstein 1965), books have been written (Wolpe 1958, Eysenck 1960, Ullman and Krasner 1965, Wolpe, Salter, and Reyna 1964, Krasner and Ullman 1965, Bandura, in press), and a journal has been established (Eysenck 1963). All report near perfect success with "behavior therapy," as it has come to be called. Even though the majority of these papers are based upon uncontrolled clinical reports, with the same problems of inadequate criteria and possible lack of comparability across populations noted in outcome reports for traditional psychotherapy, they also represent the only data available on behavior therapy. Whereas the overall "success" rate for traditional psychotherapies has been calculated at about 50 per cent, the "success" rate for reports of behavior therapy in the literature run from 80 to 95 per cent (Wolpe 1960, 1961, Eysenck 1960, 1961b, Lazarus 1963, Rachman 1963). Likewise, the comparable percentage for systematic desensitization in the present study was 100 per cent—very close to the other findings, considering the relative crudeness of all such percentage classifications and comparisons. Thus it appears that the bulk of evidence existing in the literature favors the superiority of direct treatment based upon principles of learning over traditional "depth" approaches; and the results of the present study, which was carried out under controlled conditions, provide added support.

Even though it is still possible to present logical arguments for obtained results from the conceptual viewpoints of the proponents of either the "learning" or the "disease" model, Bandura (1961) points out that the real question is which of the two approaches is more useful in generating effective procedures for modifying human behavior. As the data presented above indicate, the existing evidence is very much on the side of the learning approach. However, those therapists who are committed to the "disease" model have seriously questioned the meaningfulness of such obtained behavioral changes. Bookbinder (1962) has been the most direct in expressing criticism of re-educative approaches. Basing his arguments on the traditional conception of maladaptive behavior as a symptomatic, distorted discharge of accumulated tension that is a derivative of unconscious conflicts between contradictory impulses striving for discharge, and defensive forces, Bookbinder charges that behavior therapy is superficial at best, and possibly harmful because of the danger of "symptom substitution." He further argues that the basic agents of change in the re-educative approach are suggestion and transference, and therefore unlikely to produce lasting effects.

As Grossberg (1964) states, it is logically impossible to prove that suggestion does not play a part in eliminating maladaptive behavior, or that symptom substitution does not occur. This is especially true when the prediction of symptom substitution is phrased in such terms as "sooner or later" (Fenichel 1945). In the present study an attempt was made to obtain evidence that would at least suggest the presence or absence of symptom substitution by including scales in the follow-up battery that would allow for an indication of such changes if the process were operating. If the effects obtained by any of the treatment procedures were due to a "repression of symptoms" in order to please the therapist in the transference relationship, "the pressure of the repressed will necessarily be increased and sooner or later new symptoms will be formed. It may be, however, that the new symptoms are limited to the patients becoming more afraid, more introverted, more rigid, more dependent on the doctor" (Fenichel 1945). Therefore the traditional conceptualization does provide a specific statement of the minimal effects of symptom substitution to be expected if insight into the "underlying conflict" is not achieved—an increase in anxiety, introversion, rigidity, or dependency. On the other hand, the learning approach predicts no change in behaviors that are not specifically the focus of treatment, except in the case of behavior that could be changed by generalization to similar situations, or in the case of behavior that had previously been inhibited by the "target" behaviors. That is, from the learning framework, without provision for substitution of symptoms *in this case,* successful reduction in performance anxiety in the speech situation might be expected to lead to the subjects becoming, if anything, *less* anxious, introverted, rigid, and dependent.

The data presented earlier on changes in anxiety scores based upon additional interpersonal-evaluative situations (Table 13) failed to reveal any significant increase in anxiety for either the desensitization or the attention-placebo group, an increase that might have been expected on the basis of the symptom-substitution hypothesis. In fact, the lack of significant differences between groups argues that the anxiety reduction was specifically related to the area treated, and the relative order of obtained reductions remains consistent with that achieved in the speech situation, suggesting that some degree of generalization was achieved. Secondly, the data on extroversion-introversion, and general anxiety (Table 15), also fails to support the symptom-substitution hypothesis, with all contact groups obtaining higher extroversion scores, and desensitization and attention-placebo groups reporting greater reductions in general anxiety. No specific data are available on rigidity and dependency formulations; however, it may be noted that only one subject in each of the three treatment groups attempted to contact his therapist during the six months following treatment termination. Furthermore, the examples of improvement in other areas given by the subjects in both the desensitization and attention-placebo group suggest that they had become more open in other situations rather than more rigid.

Thus the results of the present investigation, although limited to short-term follow-up, give no support at all to the symptom-substitution hypothesis in the treatment of maladaptive anxiety. Furthermore, those reviewers who have addressed themselves to the question of symptom substitution have unanimously agreed that available evidence, including long-term follow-ups, fails to support the inevitability of substitute symptoms. The conclusions of Grossberg (1964) are representative. After finding only three cases (out of thousands surveyed) suggesting substitution of symptomatology, he concluded, "The overwhelming evidence of the present review is that therapy directed at elimination of maladaptive behavior ("symptoms") is successful and long lasting. . . . Unfortunately, psychotherapists seem to have stressed the hypothetical dangers of only curing the symptoms, while ignoring the very real dangers of the harm that is done by not curing them."

Bookbinder stated that the agent of change in behavior therapy is primarily suggestion and transference, and that therefore it is unlikely to produce lasting effects. However, the data comparing the desensitization group with the attention-placebo group argues for the specific effect of the desensitization procedure. It should be noted also that the effects of both these procedures, as well as those of the insight treatment, appear to be maintained at follow-up. This finding is in agreement with the work of the group at Phipps Clinic (Frank 1961) who found gains effected with inactive placebos to be maintained over a five-year follow-up; in other words, even when initial changes are attributed to suggestion, they may be long lasting, depending in large part upon the extent to which the changes are supported by the client's subsequent life experiences. Further tentative support of the "real" effects of suggestion is provided by reports of the success of hypnotherapy (Brenman and Gill 1947), and more recently by reports of Soviet psychotherapy. Although no means of evaluating the Soviet reports are available, Platonov (1959) claims an overall improvement rate of 94 per cent (78 per cent "success" as previously defined) using, almost exclusively, direct or indirect suggestion and persuasion.

Even granting a "real" effect for suggestion, the specific effects of desensitization appear to contribute a more direct modification of emotional reactions, leading to a greater reduction in anxiety than could be attributed to changes in attitudes and expectancies alone. Not only did the subjects in the desensitization group show less observable behavior characteristic of anxiety following treatment, but this group was the only one that produced a significant change in physiological arousal under stress conditions.

Some of the strongest evidence of specificity of desensitization effects over and above suggestion effects comes from a recent study of Lang and Lazovik (1963). In an excellent experimental approach to the delineation of influencing agents, these authors treated a number of college students with desensitization. By testing the effects with observable behavioral criteria (approaching and handling a phobic object, a live snake) at intervals following initial interviews and assignment, hypnosis and relaxation training, and desensitization proper, the only significant reduction in phobic behavior and accompanying anxiety was found after desensitization proper. Control subjects were exposed to the snake an equal number of times, but showed no reduction in phobic behavior. Therefore Lang and Lazovik concluded that the specific effect could be attributed to the association of cues in desensitization, and not to the suggestion effects of undergoing training, etc. Recent case reports by Paul (1964), in which external evidence of anxiety reduction was available, found that behavioral changes follow rather closely the completed items in the hierarchy; these reports, and a similar report by Wolpe (1962b), again argue for specificity of effect over and above suggestion. In these three reports with external evidence, the effects were not only found to be maintained on follow-ups of 6 months to 2 years, but also to produce additional improvements. Numerous reports in the literature on the use of systematic desensitization with more severe "neurotic" disturbances claim less than a one per cent relapse rate in follow-ups of 2 to 15 years. (Wolpe 1961, 1962a, Lazarus 1963, Rachman 1963), thus adding considerable support to the findings of the short-term follow-up of the present investigation.

There is, then, no evidence from this investigation, or from any similar investigation carried out with any degree of control, that supports the claims of the proponents of the "disease" model. As Bandura (1961) concludes, "On the whole the evidence . . . suggests that no matter what the origin of the maladaptive behavior may be, a change in behavior brought about through learning procedures may be all that is necessary for the alleviation of most forms of emotional disorders."

In contrast to the relatively high degree of anxiety reduction achieved by all three treatment groups, and the somewhat questionable degree of reduction achieved by the no-treatment controls, the no-contact controls, unaware of their participation, showed essentially no change that could not be attributed simply to the effects of taking the same battery of scales twice (Windle 1954, 1955). In the absence of treatment, the additional practice and experience of a semester speech course does not appear to have yielded any significant change either in the personalities of the individuals or in the degree of anxiety they experienced. This is supported not only by the lack of change in the no-contact controls, who actually increased on several anxiety scales, but also by the scores for the overall population at the beginning and end of the semester (Appendix J). Persons in the speech field, using psychometrically sophisticated instruments, have also conducted well controlled studies in this area. They, too, have failed to find significant changes in experienced anxiety as a result of participation in the kind of speech course usually conducted in a major university (Barnes 1961).

An Explanation of Effects

The pioneering efforts of Watson and Raynor (1920) and Guthrie (1938) in the investigation of the acquisition of maladaptive emotional reactions and behaviors, and the early studies of Mowrer (1939) and Miller (1948) on the drive properties of learned anxiety as related to neurotic reactions, culminated in Dollard and Miller's (1950) systematic development of a theory of personality development in general, and neurotic behavior in particular. Perhaps Dollard and Miller's major contribution was the hypothesis that covert behaviors, or higher mental processes such as thoughts, ideas, and images, are subject to the same principles of learning as overt behaviors. By drawing attention to the fact that social interactions could provide both cues and reinforcement, much of the maladaptive behavior seen in clinical settings could be understood in terms of learning principles.

More recently, systematic theoretical works based upon empirical research have encompassed a wide range of human behavior within a learning framework. Of particular importance to "psychopathology" are the works of Mednick (1958) on the development of schizophrenic symptomatology, Bandura and Walters (1963) on social learning and imitation, Brown (1961) and Hunt (1963) on motivation, Eriksen (1963) on perception, Becker (1963) on discipline, and Eriksen (in preparation) on defense mechanisms. In an excellent review article, Wilson (1963) surveys the literature on clinical studies of human "behavior pathology," and integrates major features of neurotic behavior with laboratory studies on experimental neuroses, conflict, frustration, and traumatic avoidance learning. In his conclusion he states: "In combination, the clinical and experimental research raises the possibility that the same principles control behavior pathology in more than one species. The unique features of human pathology seem to be traceable to the complex cognitive processes through which the problem is expressed, rather than a fundamental difference in how the pathology originates. We would tentatively conclude that the indispensable feature of pathology is a strong anxiety reaction keyed to significant aspects of the individual's experience."

With respect to the present study, we might briefly consider the possible development of maladaptive anxiety, with special reference to interpersonal-performance anxiety. Although granting the probability that constitutional factors (perhaps in the nature of neural organizations) could provide a low tolerance for stress, the basic assumption of a learning model is that strong emotional reactions can be acquired. In addition, many anxiety states seen in the clinic, especially in children, would not be viewed as a result of inappropriate learning, but as a reaction to environmental factors. Such "reactive anxiety" could result from a wide range of environmental events: sensory or stimulus deprivation; pain, punishment, or negative reinforcement; loss of customary support; trauma; disconfirmation of expectancies; and prolonged stress or physical disability. If the environmental factors are known, these anxiety states are seldom considered to be "irrational."

However, for the individuals or behaviors usually considered irrational or neurotic, anxiety may be related to inappropriate or maladaptive learning in three basic ways. First, anxiety may itself be a learned reaction in which previously neutral cues or cue complexes become associated with anxiety in a manner analogous to the classical conditioning paradigm. In this instance, anxiety might be the major feature of maladaptive behavior, inappropriately occurring when the original or related stimuli are present, usually at the mediational level.

Second, inappropriate learning may result in behavioral deficits or maladaptive behaviors (including ideas, attitudes, and expectancies), which in turn produce anxiety as a reaction to the ineffective way these behaviors operate in meeting the individual's physical and social environment. In this case, either the reactive anxiety or the maladaptive behaviors, or both, may be the prominent presenting problem.

Third, anxiety may be related to inappropriate learning in cases in which maladaptive behaviors are learned and maintained via anxiety reduction. This would include those maladaptive behaviors usually considered defense mechanisms, although the anxiety that initially maintained the behaviors may drop out, and the maladaptive behaviors may come to appear relatively "functionally autonomous."

Of course in the "real world" these specific factors seldom, if ever, exist in isolation. In fact, all of the above operations may usually be considered to interact in "spiral progression," to use Mednick's term. That is, the anxiety produced by environment, cues, or maladaptive behavior tends to generalize even further as a result of the evocation of behaviors or responses which themselves become cues for anxiety, producing more anxiety for the individual, and so forth. With stimulus and response generalization at the mediational level, and progressions similar to those involved in higher-order conditioning, we can account for not only the widespread occurrence of anxiety reactions but also the production and stability of secondary symptomatology through anxiety reduction and association. Furthermore, if one takes into account the fact that maladaptive behavior is usually intermittently reinforced, and that "reality testing" is often slight because of the reinforcing effects of avoidance behavior, one can explain the slight adaptation or extinction of such reactions in the life situation.

Viewing interpersonal-performance anxiety from this framework, we could expect original anxiety to be associated with any or all of the three basic dimensions that appear in the interpersonal-performance situation. These three dimensions are: (1) the occasion of being evaluated, (2) the presence of other persons, and (3) verbal production. The relative level of introversion and anxiety in other interpersonal and evaluative situations reported by the subjects is in agreement with this formulation.

It might also be expected that the degree of anxiety associated with the speech situation, as a prototypic stress condition, would be a function of the degree of correspondence along the stimulus generalization gradients of each of the three dimensions. Anxiety would then be most severe in those instances in which the original cues for all three gradients were concordant, i.e., trauma in a previous speaking situation. Since only persons high on performance anxiety were seen, no final conclusions can be drawn from the present study; but the majority of subjects could relate the occurrence of performance anxiety to relatively specific interpersonal, evaluative situations in which verbal production played a major role.

In addition, the great majority of subjects reported a long history of avoiding speech and other interpersonal-performance situations, a finding that is consistent with the conception of avoidance behavior as reinforcing. A number of control subjects even dropped the speech course. The fact that all subjects knew that they had to complete the public speaking course in order to graduate—and presumably also knew that their feelings and behavior were not consistent with those of other students at the University—would further increase their anxiety; therefore, avoidance behavior was thwarted, and anxiety increased through approach-avoidance conflict.

Because of the "necessary" enrollment in the speech course, given the anxiety previously associated with interpersonal performance, the situation becomes analogous to Miller's (1959) conflict model. Because man is a time-binding organism, the anxiety previously associated with interpersonal-performance situations becomes progressively more intense as he moves up the stimulus generalization gradient toward the threatening situation; additionally, the anticipation of such a situation, often cued by his own behavior or internal responses, tends to increase his anxiety as he moves closer in time and space to the appointed speech presentation. Thus, as the conflict model assumes, the "avoidance gradient" would be steeper than the "approach gradient," which may also be raised by the additional motivation provided by an instructor and by the desire to obtain approval and reward from the audience, thereby increasing the conflict.

From this framework, the events that took place in the five groups of the present study may logically be considered relative to the obtained effects. The subjects in the no-contact control group took no part in the experiment other than completing the pretreatment and follow-up test batteries. Therefore, any effects obtained for this group would be the result of participation in the speech course, which involved training and instruction in public speaking skills, listening to speeches, and presenting six speeches over the course of a five-month period. These subjects reported essentially no change in performance anxiety (Fig. 2), a finding which suggests that the focus on increasing skills (operant behavior) alone was not effective in reducing their experience of anxiety. It would be expected that continued practice in public speaking, with reinforcement from the audience, would eventually effect anxiety reduction. In the present case, however, it appears that the distributed practice in speaking may have served only to reinforce and maintain anxiety previously attendant on the speaking situation. The degree of anxiety anticipated and experienced by these individuals, combined with a probable lack of response from the audience, would only serve to reinforce avoidance of speaking situations, and prevent the logical consideration of means of overcoming the emotional reaction. Therefore, in the absence of prior alleviation of anxiety, the increased positive motivation and training in speaking skills available in the usual academic speech course appeared to be ineffective.

The subjects in the no-treatment control group received additional attention from the investigator in terms of at least one telephone contact, a short interview, participation in the two stress speeches, and a promise of treatment in the future. As previously indicated, there is some question about the interpretation of the improvement reported by this group at follow-up. However, it would appear that any effects obtained for these subjects can be attributed to the reassurance, implicit in the interactions with the investigator, that their anxiety was not unique and that it could be overcome relatively easily. Because statements or implications made by other "experts" in an individual's past history have usually been confirmed, the implicit reassurance by the investigator might be expected to change a subject's expectancies and attitudes toward his behavior in the same manner. Furthermore, this possible change in attitude might be expected to limit the "spiral progression" of anxiety in the speaking situation. Some anxiety reduction might also result from the restriction of alternative, possibly irrational, formulations developed by the subject to account for his behavior. Once some degree of anxiety reduction had been achieved, practice and instruction in speech skills might be expected to bring about additional confidence and anxiety reduction.

The self-report measures of the three formal treatment groups are less in question because of the observable effects obtained under stress conditions. The nonspecific effects of treatment obtained for the attention-placebo procedure are perhaps the most interesting because these effects appear to account for approximately 50 per cent of the overall "success rate" for desensitization, and almost all of the "success rate" for the interview approach. The "active" ingredient of the so-called placebo effect, which is present in any therapeutic undertaking, has been referred to as something "inherent in the doctor-patient relationship" (Shapiro 1959). In fact, as Shapiro points out, the great lesson of medical history is "that the placebo has always been the norm of medical practice." Wolf (1959) even states that this nebulous "placebo effect" of treatment is powerful enough to override, or even reverse, the effects of pharmacologically active drugs.

In addition to the attitudinal changes that might result from testing and the pretreatment interview, a number of factors appear to be involved in these "nonspecific" treatment effects. A subject could be motivated to actively instigate beneficial behaviors (for example, spending more time preparing for a speech) as a result of his participation in the interesting and novel procedures encountered in the testing and treatment situations (Hunt 1963). Furthermore, major changes in expectancy and attitudes toward the emotional reaction, as suggested above for the no-treatment control group, may be heightened by acceptance for treatment by a prestigeful, culturally defined "healer" of such problems (Frank 1961). The act of entering treatment may thus heighten the expectation of relief, and result in anxiety reduction because of previous experiences in which expected results were obtained from culturally defined experts.

Within the treatment setting, the subject is provided with a rationale that "explains" the experienced anxiety, and implicitly or explicitly, the "proper" way to overcome it. This may also bring a degree of relief, both by heightening the subject's expectation of benefit and by eliminating his own less adaptive alternative formulations. In the present study, as in most psychotherapeutic approaches, after the formal inception of treatment, there is a period of time in which a specific approach or "ritual" is undertaken with the intention of bringing relief to the client. As is usually the case in all approaches, the therapist maintains a warm, attentive, and interested attitude. Both Krasner (1955) and Skinner (1953) have referred to such attentional behaviors as a "generalized reinforcer." During an individual's past history, attention from other people has been a necessary precondition for specific rewards and reinforcements. Because positive reinforcements have usually been associated with a warm, interested social-reinforcing agent, the same kind of behavior from another person may come to elicit feelings of comfort and relief from distressing emotions.

An additional feature, often overlooked, existing in the attention-placebo treatment or any treatment, is the role of the therapist as a model of a calm, confident individual (Bandura and Walters 1963). Some support for the operation of such imitative behavior was evident in the present study in the significant correlation between the therapists' self-ratings of comfort and the change in the subjects' physiological composite. This was the only variable of all therapist and client ratings, and personality scales, found to be significantly related to physiological change. Considerable research evidence supports the validity of the hypothesis that the combined features of warmth, attention, and interest from a prestigeful person, combined with modeling effects, do produce change (Bandura 1956, Parloff 1956, Sapolsky 1960, Krasner 1962). Regarding modeling effects, Bandura (1961) points out that these "affectional rewards increase the secondary reinforcing properties of the model, and thus predispose the imitator to pattern his behavior after the rewarding person."

Of course, these factors are the major variables in the "therapeutic relationship" that theorists such as Rogers (1951, 1957) have talked about for years. From a learning framework, however, these factors may be viewed as possibly necessary, but not entirely sufficient, conditions for bringing about therapeutic change, even though they may account for the main effects in the majority of traditional "depth" therapies. Evidence is beginning to accumulate which shows that therapists do differ in their ability to provide these factors in the therapy setting (Betz and Whitehorn 1956, Bandura 1956, Strupp 1960, Truax 1963). The fact that all participating therapists in the present study were considered capable of establishing a warm therapeutic relationship may partially account for the overall degree of improvement obtained, particularly for the results in the attention-placebo treatment.

Two major principles of learning are believed to operate in reducing anxiety in the usual interview procedures employed in insight-oriented treatment, in addition to the common nonspecific factors discussed above—discrimination learning, and extinction or counterconditioning (Shoben 1949, Dollard and Miller 1950, Murray 1963a, Goodstein 1965). By helping clients to discriminate aspects of their own feelings and behavior in relation to the realities of the current situation, overgeneralization may be halted, and more rational approaches considered. Extinction or counterconditioning of anxiety related to interpersonal performance would be expected to take place as the client talks about anxiety-producing material within the relaxed, nonthreatening therapeutic atmosphere. While these specific "active" ingredients in interview therapy are consistent with established principles of learning, the comparative results between the insight and attention-placebo groups suggest that little additional anxiety reduction was achieved by use of these methods in the time-limited treatment period of the present study. If this treatment had been extended in time, specific effects might have been obtained; however, looking at the effects obtained with systematic desensitization, such a continuance would appear to be a very inefficient use of client and therapist time.

The systematic-desensitization treatment also includes all of the nonspecific factors discussed above in conjunction with the attention-placebo treatment (see pp. 86–88). The specific factors involved appear to be the same principles—discrimination learning and counterconditioning—believed to be operating in the interview procedure, but applied in a more direct and efficient manner. Discrimination learning would take place in the construction of the anxiety hierarchy, a process that brings the client to focus on cues and situations associated with interpersonal-performance anxiety. This focus usually leads to the discrimination of similarities and differences between feelings and events, in much the same way that interview techniques are assumed to do so.

The fact that desensitization was more efficient in alleviating anxiety may be attributed to the more controlled and focused nature of the learning situation. Instead of allowing the client to introduce haphazardly, with varying degrees of attention, symbolic anxiety-generating cues, the desensitization procedure attempts to systematically arrange the learning contingencies. Competing stimuli and responses are reduced to a minimum. The situation is constructed to limit external stimuli; and through the relaxation procedure, internal and proprioceptive stimuli are brought to a minimum. With the decrease in competing events, the therapist can direct the client's attention specifically to the cues of prime importance. By carefully controlling the client's mediating cognitive events, it is possible to progress systematically up the stimulus generalization gradient (hierarchy), always insuring that relaxation is stronger than the anxiety associated with the cues involved. Through the combination of adaptation and counterconditioning, the meaning and expectations associated with these cues come to be associated more with relaxation than with anxiety. Once a degree of anxiety reduction has been attained, the instruction, practice, and reinforcement within the speech situation can be expected to lead to an even greater reduction.

Implications for Research and Practice

The results of the present investigation strongly demonstrate the necessity of including a control for nonspecific treatment effects in the evaluation of specific therapeutic procedures. A minimum requirement for outcome research focusing on any specific treatment approach would be the inclusion of at least two types of treatment procedures with a no-treatment control, or a single treatment procedure with a "placebo" control. These requirements are particularly important in view of the increased focus on process studies by large scale researchers. Outcome effects must be evaluated to determine which procedures are most effective in application prior to, or in conjunction with, process studies. Otherwise, we may find that much of the money spent on process research, to use Cronbach's analogy, will lead only to a greater knowledge of the manner in which a "losing horse" runs.

Do no-treatment control groups actually constitute therapy groups? The findings of this study suggest that they do. However, these findings should not lead to the exclusion of no-treatment controls, since any treatment "worth its salt" should produce measurable changes over and above the effects of testing and intake procedures. The feasibility of having the same therapists work with different procedures was also demonstrated, although future studies might consider extending the training period for "placebo" treatments to further reduce therapist anxiety.

The necessity of including criterion measures of improvement from sources other than the involved participants (therapists and clients) was also evident. External behavioral criteria did, in fact, appear to be the most useful, and certainly the most reliable. However, continued use of self-report and multiple criteria is still necessary in outcome studies. Although the physiological measures used in this study were rather crude, Lacey's (1959) admonition not to rely on any single physiological measure was definitely supported. In addition, the present investigation demonstrates that there is greater concordance between criteria when the behavior and stimulus conditions in which the clients are expected to function are well specified, a finding that is especially significant for physiological and rating data. Under specified conditions, experienced therapists were able to make fairly accurate assessments of specific improvement.

In general, the design and "target behaviors" included in the present investigation appear to provide a feasible model for investigating the effectiveness and parameters of procedures directed at the alleviation of maladaptive anxiety. The major instruments used are precise enough to allow, and in fact call for, replication with a different sample of clients and therapists. With additional funds and a larger staff, the two major limitations of the present study could be overcome by (1) training speech instructors to use rating procedures and to adhere to an experimental design, in order to obtain outside measures of effectiveness, and (2) by including behavioral criteria in both short-term and long-term follow-ups.

The failure of treatment techniques based on the "disease model" of emotional disturbance to produce any greater anxiety reduction than that produced by nonspecific effects has important implications for practice. Perhaps even the terms traditionally used, such as "mental illness," "cure," "therapy," and other disease analogies, are out of place in reference to problems that may be primarily due to stress and inappropriate learning. In view of the failure of traditional treatments to make major inroads in the alleviation of maladaptive behaviors and emotional disturbances, a shift in emphasis along the lines of emotional re-education and behavioral retraining seems most promising.

An approach to the treatment of emotional disturbances similar to the one used by Kirk (1962) with retardates might result in the greatest "payoff" for time invested. Such an approach is also advocated by Bandura (in press). One would have to identify and describe presenting behavior, and then specify the objectives of treatment in terms of the desired terminal behavior and in terms of the environmental conditions in which the behavior would be expected to occur. The treatment program would then work toward these objectives (in sequential order), making use of any and all known principles of learning to achieve these specific ends. Of course a great deal of skill is needed to apply these principles to clinical problems, and the "art" of treatment must bridge the gap between empirical findings and the necessities of an individual case. There are disagreements among learning theorists, but these are primarily academic. As Osgood (1953) and Hilgard (1956) both point out, the majority of empirical findings on principles and techniques of learning are well agreed upon. A wealth of knowledge from social psychology and from learning and motivation laboratories is awaiting application to clinical problems.

As Bandura (1961) has recognized, treatment procedures derived from learning theory have unfortunately taken on "school" characteristics. The current stress on a few principles at the expense of others will only serve to limit the effectiveness of treatment. And, as Lazarus (1963) points out, behavior therapists tend to overreact against traditional procedures, and may overlook important influencing aspects. Vested interests within the ranks of those interested in applying principles of learning to clinical problems have resulted in the appearance of various camps, such as "biotropic" vs. "sociotropic" (Murray 1963b), "mechanotropic" (Shoben 1963), and "direct" vs. "indirect" (Goodstein 1965), which have no place in the application of knowledge in a clinical setting.

As an example of the limitations of "school" approaches, students of operant conditioning procedures often take Eysenck's (1959) statement, "Get rid of the symptom and you have eliminated the neurosis," at face value, without taking into account his later qualification of including causally related emotional drives. Thus, from the general theoretical framework presented in the previous section, one could expect therapeutic success in the case of "functionally autonomous" behaviors, and maladaptive motoric or instrumental behaviors resulting from inappropriate learning. However, in those instances in which the "symptom" is maintained by anxiety reduction, other behavior, which may be either adaptive or maladaptive, can be expected. In those cases in which anxiety, or any other strong emotional reaction, is involved in the overall picture as a concomitant of other maladaptive behaviors, an operant approach might eventually work, but would be much less efficient than other procedures.

To give an example particularly relevant to the present study: a focus on anxiety reduction to the exclusion of other maladaptive or deficient skills and behaviors would be considered complete only in those cases in which anxiety is a learned reaction inappropriately evoked by cues, or in those cases in which reactive anxiety results from environmental stress. As Goodstein notes, any case in which anxiety is prominent may best be handled by first alleviating that anxiety. However, the reduction of anxiety does not directly, or invariably, lead to an adaptive change in the inappropriate behaviors that may have produced anxiety initially, nor does it lead to the development of the responses or skills that have been blocked by anxiety. In these instances, the reduction of anxiety only makes the client "teachable"; the modification of other attitudes, behaviors, and skills may still require specific learning experiences.

Fortunately, the emergent behaviors in this particular study are regarded as socially appropriate, and likely to be rewarded. Furthermore, the instruction and training received in the speech course very possibly supplemented the treatment procedures in the teaching of specific skills. Thus, in practice, the systematic-desensitization procedure should provide an efficient and useful treatment technique in almost any case in which anxiety is prominent. In many instances, however, additional work would be necessary to prevent a re-establishment of anxiety through the perpetuation of other maladaptive attitudes and behaviors.

Here, something should be said about the duration of treatment in this study. Treatment was limited to five sessions, certainly a very small number when compared with the usual number of sessions reported in the literature. In representative clinic populations, where maladaptive behaviors and emotional reactions are more widespread and severe, treatment would of course take longer. However, it should be noted that the interpersonal-performance anxiety which constituted the target behavior in the present study was not as circumscribed as it might appear to be. In fact, this emotional reaction should not be considered a phobia or anxiety-hysteria, as it would be in the traditional diagnostic schema; the sample of subjects consisted of anxious-introverts, who were therefore more likely to be psychasthenics than hysterics (Eriksen

1963); the anxiety experienced by these subjects was not specific only to "speeches," "crowds," or "stages"; it was a more generalized reaction to interpersonal-evaluative situations (Table 13). These relationships have previously been noted by Law and Sheets (1951) who found that the students who scored highest on performance anxiety in the speaking situation obtained significantly higher scores on the K, Pt, and D scales of the MMPI than a low-anxiety group; the high-anxiety group was also found to be generally less adjusted socially.

Many problems brought to a clinic or a university counseling bureau are very much like the problems involved in this study, and in many cases they may be successfully dealt with in no more than three to four sessions of focalized treatment based on learning principles (Paul 1964). Frank (1961) points out that the average number of treatment sessions at counseling bureaus in 1949 was six, but that in following years the number gradually lengthened to thirty. As Frank (1959b) has mentioned in relation to traditional psychotherapy, "Those who practice long-term psychotherapy find that their patients take a long time to respond; those who believe that good results can be produced in a few weeks claim to obtain them in this period of time. There is no evidence that a larger proportion of patients in long-term treatment improve, or that the improvements are more permanent than in patients treated more briefly. On the other hand, there is some experimental evidence that patients respond more promptly when they know in advance that therapy is "time-limited."

As in the present study, previous literature seems to find that therapist ratings are the only "evidence" calling for lengthy treatment of problems of a neurotic nature (Lorr 1962). Even in those situations in which long-term treatment is favored, short-term treatment is more likely. Strupp (1962b), for example, reports that a "large proportion" of patients at the psychiatric outpatient clinic of the North Carolina Memorial Hospital are seen for less than five times after diagnostic workup.

Shlien, Mosak, and Dreikers (1960) report that both client-centered therapy and Adlerian psychotherapy, limited to a maximum of 20 sessions, were found to be not only as effective but also twice as efficient as unlimited client-centered therapy, as indicated by self-ideal discrepancy. More importantly, these authors found a significant improvement at the seventh session (first measuring period) for both time-limited groups, and found no change at all for the unlimited-treatment group. More recently, Muench (1964) has reported that the improvement recorded on self-report adjustment measures by 35 counseling-bureau clients whose treatment was limited to 8 sessions was significantly greater than the improvement reported by a similar group of 35 long-term (>20 sessions) clients. Thus it seems that, even with traditional interview procedures, treatment need not extend indefinitely.

Lazarus (1963) reports a mean of 14.07 sessions necessary for the treatment of "most difficult" or severe neuroses by means of learning procedures focusing on cognitive events within the context of a warm, sympathetic therapeutic relationship. Another very interesting report along these lines appeared some years ago. Pascal (1947) presented a number of cases treated by procedures very similar to the desensitization approach, although he viewed the technique as a "rapid method of getting at repressed areas." In nine of the cases reported, anxiety was a predominant problem; Pascal reported complete success with these cases in an average of 5.6 sessions.

In general we may conclude that the majority of cases currently seen in clinics and counseling bureaus, especially those in which anxiety is a prominent problem, may be treated effectively by re-educative procedures in a relatively short period of time. It should also be noted that many clients may expect, or even demand, a rational formulation of their difficulties (Frank 1961), which could then be included as a part of structuring for treatment. However, the most promising approach to the application of empirical knowledge to clinical problems should follow the guide, stated by Kalish (1965), ". . . in therapy as in experiments, the problem should dictate the procedure."

I would like to conclude with a paraphrase of Frank's (1963) warning to the practitioner. To achieve any sort of success with the application of learning procedures, either the therapist or his advisor must be thoroughly familiar with two aspects of the total problem that exist apart from his client and the intricacies of the disturbance he is attempting to treat: principles of learning, and the necessity to be rigorous in their application. To quote: "This rigor is not intended to gainsay the very real value of insight and the 'hunch,' but merely to insure that available knowledge is effectively applied, that existing techniques are meaningfully evaluated, and that new inspirations are given the maximum opportunity to demonstrate their value."

SUMMARY AND CONCLUSIONS

This study was concerned with the controversy between "insight" and "behavioral" approaches in the field of psychotherapy. After a discussion of the methodological and control problems that restrict pure field studies, interpersonal-performance anxiety was offered as a research focus delimited enough to allow rigorous experimental methodology, but important enough to allow far-reaching generalization of findings.

Taking the public-speaking situation as a prototypic stress condition for the elicitation of interpersonal-performance anxiety, a comparative investigation of "insight" and "behavioral" treatments was conducted, within a model that demanded more rigorous controls and more objective criteria than had previously been attained in outcome research. Specific objectives were: (a) to compare the relative efficacy of treatment based on the traditional "disease" model of emotional disturbance (insight-oriented psychotherapy) and treatment based on a "learning" model of emotional disturbance (modified systematic desensitization) in reducing maladaptive interpersonal-performance anxiety; (b) to evaluate the contribution of the "nonspecific" effects of undergoing treatment; (c) to compare the effects of individual treatment with the effects of testing and course instruction alone; (d) to determine the degree of anxiety reduction resulting only from undergoing testing procedures and being placed on a "waiting list"; and (e) to add to the construct validation of promising measuring instruments.

A battery of personality and anxiety scales was administered to 710 speech students. Ninety-six of these students—the most debilitated by anxiety of those who requested treatment—were then selected as subjects. Cognitive, physiological, and observable behavioral measures of anxiety were obtained on 74 subjects during a pretreatment stress speech. Following a screening interview, these subjects were assigned to one of four groups, equated on observable anxiety, to receive: (a) modified systematic desensitization, (b) insight-oriented psychotherapy, (c) attention-placebo treatment, or (d) no treatment. The remaining 22 subjects constituted a no-contact control.

Five experienced psychotherapists worked individually with three subjects in each of the three treatment groups for five hours over a six-week period; posttreatment stress measures were then obtained on the treated subjects and the no-treatment controls. Follow-up measures on the test battery were obtained for all five groups six weeks later. Attitudinal and improvement ratings were obtained from subjects and therapists.

Analyses of variance and comparison of individual improvement rates found systematic desensitization consistently superior (100 per cent success); no differences were found between the effects of insight-oriented psychotherapy and the nonspecific effects of the attention-placebo treatment (47 per cent success), although both groups showed greater anxiety reduction than the no-treatment controls (17 per cent). Improvement was maintained at follow-up with no evidence of "symptom substitution." No differences were found between effects produced by different therapists, nor was improvement predictable from major personality variables.

The consistency of results with previous research was discussed, and a theoretical analysis of the role of anxiety in the development of emotional disorders was presented in terms of learning. A logical analysis of transactions in all groups was presented, and implications for research and clinical practice were discussed, resulting in the following major conclusions: (a) "psychotherapy" does produce greater measurable reduction of anxiety than no treatment; (b) a one-semester speech course does *not* result in a significant reduction of interpersonal-performance anxiety; (c) testing and initial interview procedures may produce some degree of anxiety reduction, but effective individual treatment produces greater effects; (d) at least on a short-term basis, the nonspecific factors of relationship, attention, suggestion, etc., produce as much anxiety reduction as gaining "insight" and "self-understanding"; (e) treatment based upon a learning model is most effective in alleviating anxiety of a social-evaluative nature; (f) anxiety may be reliably measured, with observable behavioral criteria being the most useful; and (g) appropriate control groups must be included in attempts to evaluate specific treatment effects.

In conclusion, the design and focus of the present study does appear to provide a feasible model for well controlled investigation of both outcome and parameters of various approaches to behavior modification. It is hoped that in the future we will see not only a needed replication of the present investigation, but also the development and testing of new treatment techniques, the effects of which may be evaluated on the basis of sound empirical findings.

APPENDIXES

A. Test-Battery Forwards

Dear Student:

Today you are being asked to complete the accompanying attitude battery in conjunction with a study we are conducting in the Department of Psychology. This study is a continuation of work that has been underway for the past two years.

Briefly, we have been concerned with the number of students who experience situational anxieties, or emotional reactions in certain situations, during their college careers and in later life that not only make them uncomfortable and less happy, but can actually lower their academic grades and restrict earning potential. These reactions have been found to exist in approximately 20 per cent of the normal student population. We have worked with several of these students using psychological principles, training, and therapeutic procedures with excellent and gratifying results.

The purpose of the present study is to determine which people benefit *most* from the specific psychological procedures involved. We are focusing specifically upon the speech situation as one in which many students feel upset, worry, and suffer from a lack of confidence that interferes with effective performance, thus lowering grades, making life more complicated, and restricting interests and earning power. You, as an individual, may or may not experience these feelings. If you do, we may be able to help you overcome them, but in any case your responses will be most helpful to us, even if you have no major difficulty with your emotional reactions as a speaker.

All students in Speech 101 are being asked to complete the attitude battery. Additionally, we will be able to meet with a number of students to help them overcome anxieties related to public speaking and obtain more confidence as a speaker. Of course, not all students will be bothered by these problems, nor will all students feel they have the time or need for these services.

On the following page, you are asked to indicate whether you would or would not be interested in obtaining help with these difficulties, and whether you have the time available to participate. Participation in this phase of the program would require approximately 7 to 8 hours during the semester. Five of these hours would be spent meeting with a trained specialist one hour per week during the latter part of the semester. These meetings will probably be in the evenings or on Saturday, depending upon your own schedule. These services normally would cost $15 to $20 per hour; however, since this study is being supported by the Department of Health, Education, and Welfare, the specialists will be paid by the Government at no cost to you. An additional 1 to 1½ hours of your time would be necessary to meet with a group of students and with me for further evaluation prior to treatment and again for 1 to 1½ hours the week immediately following the treatment period. A short interview would also be scheduled following the first evaluation to discuss the results with you. This will mean approximately 7 or 8 hours *total time* during the semester to participate in all phases.

Needless to say, your answers to the questions in the attitude battery, and participation in the other phases of the study will be kept strictly confidential; under no circumstances will they be made known to any instructor or official of the University. The general results of the study will be presented to the speech instructors *after* the semester is completed, but even here, no names will be involved.

Thank you for your cooperation.

FOLLOW-UP BATTERY COVER LETTER

Dear Student:

Today you are again being asked to complete the accompanying attitude battery in conjunction with a study we are conducting in the Department of Psychology. This is the same battery that you completed earlier in the semester.

As you may remember, the purpose of the present study is both to further our knowledge about situational anxieties, or emotional reactions in certain situations, and to determine which people benefit *most* from different types of psychological procedures found to be of help in alleviating anxieties.

We have worked with a great many of you this semester, and your responses will help us to determine which of the various procedures are most helpful for different types of people. Those of you whom we were unable to see this semester, or those of you who did not feel you had time or need for our services, will still provide us with helpful information.

Since well over 300 students indicated interest in the project, we were unable to meet with all students as we had hoped. However, if any of you still feel that you would like help in overcoming anxieties related to public speaking, you may indicate your interest on the following page, and we will contact you as time and facilities permit. Space is also provided for you to indicate if you would like to obtain the results of the test battery after we have had sufficient time to score them.

As before, your answers to the questions in the attitude battery, and interest or participation in other aspects of the study will be kept strictly confidential; under no circumstances will they be made known to any instructor or official of the University. The general results of the study will be presented to the speech instructors after the semester is completed, but even here, no names will be involved.

Thank you for your cooperation.

FOLLOW-UP BATTERY DATA SHEET

Name:_____ Age:_____ Sex:_____

Date:_____ I.D. Number:_____ Phone:_____

Class (Fresh., Soph., etc.) :_____ Major:_____

Course and Section:_____ Instructor:_____

Please answer by circling the appropriate alternatives:

1. Did you participate in the "outside" evaluation speeches of this project?
   (yes; no)
   (a) Did you find these speeches and the evaluation interview helpful?
       (not applicable; not at all; somewhat; much; very much)

2. Did you meet with someone on a regular basis, *in conjunction with this project,* to work on alleviating anxiety connected with situational stress such as public speaking?
   (yes; no)
   (a) To what degree do you feel these sessions have been helpful in over-coming anxieties related to public speaking?
       (not applicable; not at all; somewhat; much; very much)
   (b) To what degree have these sessions been helpful in other areas, in addition to the speech situation?
       (not applicable; not at all; somewhat; much; very much)
       Please indicate other situations or areas in which these meetings have helped _____
   (c) With whom did you meet? (name) _____
   (d) What is your opinion of this person?
       (incompetent; competent; very competent)
       (unlikable; likable; very likable)

3. Did you meet with anyone for help of a psychological nature during the semester, *not* in conjunction with this project?
   (yes; no) If *yes,* (name) _____

Please indicate by checking (a) or (b) if appropriate. Remember that your answers are completely confidential.
   _____(a) I would like to meet with someone next semester to work on over-coming emotional reactions attendant upon public speaking.
   _____(b) I would like to obtain the results of this test battery. (If you are interested in obtaining these results, call 333-0040 the latter part of February to arrange for an appointment.)

B. New Performance-Anxiety Instruments

This instrument is composed of 30 items regarding your feelings of confidence as a speaker. After each question there is a "true" and a "false."

Try to decide whether "true" or "false" *most* represents your feelings associated with your *most recent* speech, then put a *circle around* the "true" or "false." Remember that this information is completely confidential and will not be made known to your instructor. *Work quickly* and don't spend much time on any one question. We want your *first impression* on this questionnaire. Now go ahead, work quickly, and remember to answer every question.

1. I look forward to an opportunity to speak in public. T F
2. My hands tremble when I try to handle objects on the platform. *T* F
3. I am in constant fear of forgetting my speech. *T* F
4. Audiences seem friendly when I address them. T *F*
5. While preparing a speech I am in a constant state of anxiety. *T* F
6. At the conclusion of a speech I feel that I have had a pleasant experience. T *F*
7. I dislike to use my body and voice expressively. *T* F
8. My thoughts become confused and jumbled when I speak before an audience. *T* F
9. I have no fear of facing an audience. T *F*
10. Although I am nervous just before getting up I soon forget my fears and enjoy the experience. T *F*
11. I face the prospect of making a speech with complete confidence. T *F*
12. I feel that I am in complete possession of myself while speaking. T *F*
13. I prefer to have notes on the platform in case I forget my speech. *T* F
14. I like to observe the reactions of my audience to my speech. T *F*
15. Although I talk fluently with friends I am at a loss for words on the platform. *T* F
16. I feel relaxed and comfortable while speaking. T *F*

17. Although I do not enjoy speaking in public I do not particularly dread it.   T   *F*

18. I always avoid speaking in public if possible.   *T*   F

19. The faces of my audience are blurred when I look at them.   *T*   F

20. I feel disgusted with myself after trying to address a group of people.   T   F

21. I enjoy preparing a talk.   T   *F*

22. My mind is clear when I face an audience.   T   *F*

23. I am fairly fluent.   T   *F*

24. I perspire and tremble just before getting up to speak.   *T*   F

25. My posture feels strained and unnatural.   *T*   F

26. I am fearful and tense all the while I am speaking before a group of people.   *T*   F

27. I find the prospect of speaking mildly pleasant.   T   *F*

28. It is difficult for me to calmly search my mind for the right words to express my thoughts.   *T*   F

29. I am terrified at the thought of speaking before a group of people.   *T*   F

30. I have a feeling of alertness in facing an audience.   T   *F*

TIMED BEHAVIORAL CHECKLIST FOR
PERFORMANCE ANXIETY

Rater.................................... Name..

Date.............................. Speech No...................... I.D...............................

Behavior Observed	Time Period								
	1	2	3	4	5	6	7	8	Σ
1. Paces									
2. Sways									
3. Shuffles Feet									
4. Knees Tremble									
5. Extraneous Arm and Hand Movement (swings, scratches, toys, etc.)									
6. Arms Rigid									
7. Hands Restrained (in pockets, behind back, clasped)									
8. Hand Tremors									
9. No Eye Contact									
10. Face Muscles Tense (drawn, tics, grimaces)									
11. Face "Deadpan"									
12. Face Pale									
13. Face Flushed (blushes)									
14. Moistens Lips									
15. Swallows									
16. Clears Throat									
17. Breathes Heavily									
18. Perspires (face, hands, armpits)									
19. Voice Quivers									
20. Speech Blocks or Stammers									

Comments: Σ Σ

C. Therapist Rating Forms

The following pages contain a number of areas in which psychotherapists have been found to differ. Please indicate your position with regard to each area by placing a checkmark on the scale accompanying each area.

For example: 1. Activity-frequency.

If you feel that with *most* clients you are *usually* active (talkative), or *usually* passive, you would place the checkmark as follows:

Active.✓..|......|......|......|......Passive, or Active......|......|......|......|.✓.Passive

If you feel you are *more often* active than passive, or *more often* passive than active, you would check as follows:

Active......|.✓.|......|......|......Passive, or Active......|......|......|.✓.|......Passive

If you feel you are *about equally* active and passive with most clients, or active with as many clients as passive, you would check the middle space:

Active.......|.......|.✓...|........|.......Passive

1. Activity—frequency:

    Active.......|........|........|........|........Passive
    (Talkative)   (Nontalkative)

2. Activity—type:

    Directive.......|........|........|........|........Nondirective

3. Activity—structure:

    Informal.......|........|........|........|........Formal

4. Relationship—tenor:

    Personal.......|........|........|........|........Impersonal
    (Involved)   (Detached)

5. Relationship—structure:

    Unstructured.......|........|........|........|........Structured

6. Relationship—atmosphere:

    Permissive.......|........|........|........|........Nonpermissive

7. Relationship—therapist actions:

   Planned.......|.......|.......|.......|.......Spontaneous

8. Relationship—client dynamics:

   Nonconceptualized.......|.......|.......|.......|.......Conceptualized

9. Goals—source:

   Therapist.......|.......|.......|.......|.......Client

10. Goals—formalization:

   Planned.......|.......|.......|.......|.......Unplanned
   (Formalized)   (Unformalized)

11. Therapist Comfort and Security:

   Always Secure.......|.......|.......|.......|.......Never Secure
   (Comfortable)   (Uncomfortable)

12. Client Comfort and Security:

   Never Secure.......|.......|.......|.......|.......Always Secure
   (Uncomfortable)   (Comfortable)

13. Client Personal Growth:

   Not Inherent.......|.......|.......|.......|.......Inherent

14. Therapeutic Gains—self-understanding (cognitive insight):

   Important.......|.......|.......|.......|.......Unimportant

15. Therapeutic Gains—emotional understanding (affective awareness):

   Unimportant.......|.......|.......|.......|.......Important

16. Therapeutic Gains—"symptom" reduction:

   Important.......|.......|.......|.......|.......Unimportant

17. Therapeutic Gains—social adjustment:

   Unimportant.......|.......|.......|.......|.......Important

18. Therapeutic Gains—confidence in effecting change:

   Confident.......|.......|.......|.......|.......Unconfident

19. Learning Process in Therapy:

   Verbal-Conceptual.......|.......|.......|.......|.......Nonverbal-Affective

20. Therapeutically Significant Topics:

   Client Centered.......|.......|.......|.......|.......Theory Centered

21. Therapeutically Significant Topics:

   Historical.......|.......|.......|.......|.......Current

22. Therapeutically Significant Topics:

   Ego Functions.......|.......|.......|.......|.......Superego, Id

23. Theory of Motivation:

   Unconscious.......|.......|.......|.......|.......Conscious

24. Curative Aspect of Therapist:

   Personality.......|.......|.......|.......|.......Training

The following items refer to the use of *specific techniques* in psychotherapy. Please check to indicate whether you use each technique: almost always, usually, about half the time, only occasionally, never.

	Almost Always	50/50	Never
25. Reflection and Clarification of Feelings:			
26. Reflection and Clarification of Content:			
27. Reflection and Clarification of Behavior:			
28. Questioning of Feelings:			
29. Questioning of Content:			
30. Questioning of Behavior:			
31. Interpretation of Feelings:			
32. Interpretation of Content:			
33. Interpretation of Behavior:			
34. Suggestion (not hypnosis):			
35. Reassurance:			
36. Information and Advice Giving:			
37. Attentive Listening:			
38. Modeling Techniques (examples):			
39. Positive Attitude, Confidence:			
40. Warmth and Understanding:			
41. Reinforcement (approval-disapproval):			
42. Conditioning, Counterconditioning:			
43. Free Association:			
44. Auxiliary Techniques (hypnosis, medication):			
45. Other (please specify):			

THERAPIST PERSONAL DATA

A. Indicate in order, the *three* authors who have been most influential in shaping your *present* approach to psychotherapy.

1. ....

2. ....

3. ....

B. Indicate the "school" or "schools" of psychotherapy to which you feel *most* related.

1. ....

2. ....

C. Indicate the number of years of therapy experience you have gained to this time. ....

D. Have you obtained personal analysis and/or psychotherapy? ....
(If yes):

1. Number of sessions? ....

2. Type (*i.e.*, individual-group, analysis-client centered, etc.)

....

THERAPIST POSTTREATMENT QUESTIONNAIRE

Please complete each of the following questions for the client indicated on completion of the last treatment session.

Client:_____

1. Was this client likable?

   Very *Un*likable........|........|........|........|........Very Likable

2. Was this client responsive to treatment?

   Very *Un*responsive........|........|........|........|........Very Responsive

3. Was treatment of appropriate *length* for this client to significantly reduce performance anxiety?

   Too Short........|........|........|........|........Too Long

   a. If length was inappropriate, how many sessions would you estimate to have been more appropriate?   _____sessions.

4. Was this *type* of treatment appropriate for this client for reducing performance anxiety?

   Very *In*appropriate........|........|........|........|........Very Appropriate

   a. If type was *other* than appropriate, what type of treatment would have been more appropriate?   _____

5. To what degree has this client's performance anxiety been reduced?

   None........|........|........|........|........Very Much

   a. How confident are you of this rating? $p =$ _____

6. To what degree has this client improved in areas *other* than performance anxiety?

   None........|........|........|........|........Very Much

   a. How confident are you of this rating? $p =$ _____

7. Is further treatment indicated for this client for performance anxiety?

   Not At All........|........|........|........|........Strongly Indicated

8. Is further treatment indicated for this client in areas *other* than performance anxiety?

   Not At All........|........|........|........|........Strongly Indicated

9. Did you feel comfortable working with this form of treatment with this client?

   Very *Un*comfortable........|........|........|........|........Very Comfortable

10. Any further comments you wish to make: _____

D. Systematic Desensitization Treatment Manual

This treatment is basically the Systematic Desensitization Therapy of Wolpe, with several modifications directed toward reducing the number of sessions required for anxiety reduction. There are five major procedures involved in the use of this technique: (1) exploration of history and current status of symptoms; (2) explanation of rationale; (3) construction of anxiety hierarchy; (4) training in progressive relaxation; and (5) desensitization proper—working through the hierarchy under relaxation.

Although flexibility is normally the rule with this approach, the goals of research require that all therapists follow the outlined procedures as closely as feasible. Unlike the interpretation given by several writers in the area, this procedure is *not* to be carried out as a cold, manipulative operation; instead the therapist should be as warm, interested, and helpful as he would be in any helping relationship. The main difference between this approach and more traditional methods is that the therapist *openly* guides and directs the course and content of treatment, with a minimum of time and effort spent on introspection, and little or none spent on the client's searching for etiological factors. All happenings and incidences will be interpreted within this system if questioned, and dynamics left uninterpreted unless questioned. If questioned, interpret in a *general* manner—only superficially. In any case, it is most important that the therapist remain *confident* and stay with this specific treatment. Since the "target behavior" (speech anxiety) will have been determined prior to the therapist's contact with the client, focus on retraining will begin with the first session, with desensitization proper beginning in the second session.

The following time schedule should handle most clients.

First session:

1. Exploration of history and current status of symptoms (5–10 minutes).
2. Explanation of rationale and course of treatment (5–10 minutes).
3. Construction of anxiety hierarchy (10–15 minutes).
4. Training in progressive relaxation (20–35 minutes). Test imagery if time available.

Second to fifth sessions:

1. Check on success with relaxation and correct any problems arising (2–10 minutes).
2. Induce relaxation—present visualizations.
3. Check on images and anxiety both in treatment and outside.

SPECIFIC PROCEDURES

✳1. *Exploration of history and current status of symptoms.* For the research project, this phase will be relatively short, serving primarily as an "icebreaker" and as a period in which to establish rapport. To help describe subjects and to further therapist understanding, determine (a) *how long* the subject has experienced performance anxiety, (b) to what *degree* performance anxiety *interferes* with functioning, and (c) whether other social or evaluative situations also arouse anxiety. This should be completed in no more than 10 minutes of the first session.

2. *Explanation of rationale and course of treatment.* It is important that each subject understand and accept the treatment process. Both the theory and course of treatment should be briefly explained and repeated if questions arise. It should be made clear that the anxiety is a result of learning, and that the treatment is a learning process. If any subject seems to have trouble understanding, rephrase your explanation in language he can understand. Be sure to allay any doubts the more sophisticated subjects may have, *e.g.*, "this does *not* produce inhibitions that might lead to symptom substitution, but is desensitizing—removing the problem." The following brief explanation usually suffices for introductory purposes.

"The emotional reactions that you experience are a result of your previous experiences with people and situations; these reactions oftentimes lead to feelings of anxiety or tenseness which are really inappropriate. Since perceptions of situations occur within ourselves, it is possible to work with your reactions right here in the office by having you image or visualize those situations.

"The specific technique we will be using is one called desensitization. This technique utilizes two main procedures—relaxation and counterconditioning—to reduce your anxiety. The relaxation procedure is based upon years of work that was started in the 1930's by Dr. Jacobsen. Dr. Jacobsen developed a method of inducing relaxation that can be learned very quickly, and which will allow you to become more deeply relaxed than ever before. Of course, the real advantage of relaxation is that the muscle systems in your body cannot be both tense and relaxed at the same time; therefore, once you have learned the relaxation technique, it can be used to counter anxiety, tenseness, and feelings like those you experience in the speech situation.

"Relaxation alone can be used to reduce anxiety and tension, and I'll be asking you to practice relaxation between our meetings. Often, however, relaxation is inconvenient to use, and really doesn't permanently overcome anxiety. Therefore, we combine the relaxation technique with the psychological principle of counterconditioning to actually desensitize situations so that anxiety no longer occurs.

"The way in which we will do this is to determine the situations in which you become progressively more anxious, building a hierarchy from the least to the most anxious situations with regard to giving a speech. Then I will teach you the technique of progressive relaxation, and have you practice this. You will see how this operates in a few minutes when we actually start training. After you are more relaxed than ever before, we will then start counterconditioning. This will be done by having you repeatedly image the specific situations from the anxiety hierarchy while under relaxation. By having you visualize very briefly, while you are deeply relaxed, the situations that normally arouse anxiety, those situations gradually become desensitized, so that they no longer make you anxious. We start with those situations that bother you the least, and gradually work up to the speech itself. Since each visualization will lower your anxiety to the next, a full-fledged anxiety reaction never occurs.

"We've used these procedures on many different types of clinical problems, including several students with performance anxiety, with excellent results. Most of these procedures will become clearer after we get into them. Do you have any questions before we continue?"

3. *Construction of the anxiety hierarchy.* The anxiety hierarchy is one of the most important aspects of this treatment. The object is to determine situations related to speech presentation which run from very slight, controllable amounts of anxiety to the most extreme anxiety attendant upon the actual speech presentation. It is not necessary to determine every instance, since generalization from one instance to another will bridge the gap. It is necessary to determine situations close enough together to allow generalization to occur.

3a. *The basic speech-anxiety hierarchy.* Based upon interviews with students and analysis of the situation, the following temporal hierarchy should form the basic framework, thus reducing the time involved. The (0) item should be nonanxious and used to test imagery.

(0) Lying in bed in room just before going to sleep—describe room.
(1) Reading about speeches alone in room (one to two weeks before).
(2) Discussing coming speech a week before (in class or after).
(3) In audience while another gives speech (week before presentation).
(4) Writing speech in study area (room, library).

(5) Practicing speech alone in room (or in front of roommate).
(6) Getting dressed the morning of speech.
(7) Activities just prior to leaving for speech (eating, practice).
(8) Walking over to room on day of speech.
(9) Entering room on day of speech.
(10) Waiting while another person gives speech on day of presentation.
(11) Walking up before the audience.
(12) Presenting speech before the audience (see faces, etc.).

If time remains, presenting speeches before different and larger audiences.

This hierarchy is to serve only as a guide; each subject should have his own. The procedure is as follows. First explain that you wish to determine specific situations from the least to the most anxiety producing. Ask the subject *when* he first notices feelings of tenseness and anxiety; then work through each of the 12 items to determine if some items should be excluded or others included. *Write down* the specifics associated with each item, so that you may better control the imagery of the subject, *i.e.*, exactly where the subject studies, cues in the room, times, etc. You should have enough understanding so that, if necessary, you may "fill in" another item during desensitization without help from the subject. Most hierarchies will not be shorter than 8 items, nor longer than 12 items.

4. *Training in progressive relaxation.* This is a most important procedure, and one that should be mastered. It should be explained to the subject that this technique will take some time (20–35 minutes) at first, but as he learns, the time for inducing deep relaxation will be shortened. Training begins by having the subject systematically tense his gross-muscle systems, holding them tense until you say "relax," at which time the subject lets go immediately. If the muscles are first tensed, they will relax more deeply when they are released. Also explain that you want the subject to focus all his attention on each muscle system as you work through the various groups, so that after practice he will not have to tense the muscles first in order to achieve deep relaxation.

4a. *The Method.* Seat the subject in an overstuffed chair, with the therapist sitting slightly to one side. Legs should be extended, head resting on the back of the chair, and arms resting on the arms of the chair. No part of the body should require the use of muscles for support. Have the subject close his eyes to minimize external stimulation. The room should be quiet and lights dimmed if possible.

(1) Instruct the subject to "make a fist with your dominant hand [usually right]. Make a fist and tense the muscles of your [right] hand and forearm; tense until it trembles. Feel the muscles pull across your fingers and the lower part of your forearm." Have the subject hold this position

for 5 to 7 seconds, then say "relax," instructing him to just let his hand go: "Pay attention to the muscles of your [right] hand and forearm as they relax. Note how those muscles feel as relaxation flows through them" (10–20 seconds).

"Again, tense the muscles of your [right] hand and forearm. Pay attention to the muscles involved" (5–7 seconds). "O.K., relax; attend only to those muscles, and note how they feel as the relaxation takes place, becoming more and more relaxed, more relaxed than ever before. Each time we do this you'll relax even more until your arm and hand are completely relaxed with no tension at all, warm and relaxed."

Continue until subject reports his [right] hand and forearm are completely relaxed with no tension (usually 2–4 times is sufficient).

(2) Instruct the subject to tense his [right] biceps, leaving his hand and forearm on the chair. Proceed in the same manner as above, in a "hypnotic monotone," using the [right] hand as a reference point, that is, move on when the subject reports his biceps feels as completely relaxed as his hand and forearm.

Proceed to other gross-muscle groups (listed below) in the same manner, with the same verbalization. For example: "Note how these muscles feel as they relax; feel the relaxation and warmth flow through these muscles; pay attention to these muscles so that later you can relax them again." Always use the preceding group as a reference for moving on.

(3) Nondominant [left] hand and forearm—feel muscles over knuckles and on lower part of arm.

(4) Nondominant [left] biceps.

(5) Frown hard, tensing muscles of forehead and top of head (these muscles often "tingle" as they relax).

(6) Wrinkle nose, feeling muscles across top of cheeks and upper lip.

(7) Draw corners of mouth back, feeling jaw muscles and cheeks.

(8) Tighten chin and throat muscles, feeling two muscles in front of throat.

(9) Tighten chest muscles and muscles across back—feel muscles pull below shoulder blades.

(10) Tighten abdominal muscles—make abdomen hard.

(11) Tighten muscles of right upper leg—feel one muscle on top and two on the bottom of the upper leg.

(12) Tighten right calf—feel muscles on bottom of right calf.

(13) Push down with toes and arch right foot—feel pressure as if something were pushing up under the arch.

(14) Left upper leg.

(15) Left calf.

(16) Left foot.

For most muscle groups, two presentations will suffice. Ask the subject if he feels any tension anywhere in his body. If he does, go back and repeat the tension-release cycle for that muscle group. It is often helpful to instruct the subject to take a deep breath and hold it while tensing muscles, and to let it go while releasing. Should any muscle group not respond after four trials, move on and return to it later. *Caution:* some subjects may develop muscle cramps or spasms from prolonged tension of muscles. If this occurs, shorten the tension interval a few seconds, and instruct the subject not to tense his muscles quite so hard.

Although the word "hypnosis" is not to be used, progressive relaxation, properly executed, does seem to resemble a light hypnotic-trance state, with the subject more susceptible to suggestion. Relaxation may be further deepened by repetition of suggestions of warmth, relaxation, etc. Some subjects may actually report sensations of disassociation from their bodies. This is complete relaxation and is to be expected. Subjects should be instructed to speak as little as possible while under relaxation.

In bringing subjects back to "normal," the numerical method of trance termination should be used: "I'm going to count from one to four. On the count of one, start moving your legs; two, your fingers and hands; three, your head; and four, open your eyes and sit up. One—move your legs; two —now your fingers and hands; three—move your head around; four— open your eyes and sit up." Always check to see that the subject feels well, alert, etc., before leaving.

The subject should be instructed to practice relaxation twice a day between sessions. He should not work at it more than 15 minutes at a time, and should not practice twice within any three-hour period. He should also practice alone. Relaxation may be used to get to sleep if practiced while horizontal; if the subject does not wish to sleep, he should practice sitting up. Properly timed, relaxation can be used for a "second wind" during study.

By the third session, if the subject has been practicing well, relaxation may be induced by merely focusing attention on the muscle groups, and instructing the subject to "concentrate on muscles becoming relaxed, "warm," etc. However, if any subject has difficulty following straight suggestions, return to the use of tension-release.

5. *Desensitization proper*—working through the hierarchy under relaxation. Preparatory to desensitization proper, usually at the end of the first session, the subject's imagery should be tested. This may be done by asking him to visualize item (0): "Now visualize yourself lying in bed in your room just before going to sleep. Describe what you see. Do you see it clearly? Do you see color? Do you feel as if you were there? All right, now stop visualizing that and go on relaxing." Some subjects may report

clear, distinct images, as if they were watching a movie; this is fine, but not necessary. The minimum requirement is that their visualizations be as clear as a very vivid memory. Describing these visualizations as a dream is often helpful. With more practice, images will usually become clearer. It is also important that the subject can start and stop an image on request, and this should be determined. If difficulties arise in any of these areas, present a few more common, nonanxious images, describing for the subject just what he should experience; for example, entering the office. It is important that the subject visualize situations as if he were there—*not* watching himself!

Before inducing relaxation in the second session, explain exactly what you'll be asking the subject to do, since his verbalizations are to be kept at a minimum. Tell him that if *anytime* during the session he feels any tension or nervousness whatever, to signal by raising his [right] index finger. This is important, and should be made clear from the beginning.

After relaxation is induced, presentation of images begins with item (1). "Now I want you to visualize yourself sitting alone in your room two weeks before a speech, reading about speeches" (10 seconds). "Stop visualizing that, and go on relaxing." Ask if the subject felt any tension and if he was able to start and stop the image on request. Then repeat item (1) again. "One more time, visualize yourself, two weeks before a speech, sitting alone in your room, reading about giving a speech" (10 seconds). "Stop visualizing that, and go on relaxing—completely relaxed, no tension anywhere in your body, warm and relaxed."

Follow the above paradigm throughout the hierarchy *if the subject does not become anxious:* i.e., present each item in the hierarchy, specifying all major aspects of the image. Allow 10 seconds to elapse after each presentation, then instruct the subject to "stop visualizing that, and go on relaxing." Continue suggestions of warmth, relaxation, lack of tension, heaviness, etc. for 30 to 45 seconds, and again present the image. Present each item in the hierarchy at least twice. If the subject does not signal anxiety, and the therapist does not detect anxiety during two 10-second presentations of an item, move on to the next item in the hierarchy.

If, on the other hand, the subject signals anxiety or the therapist detects anxiety in the subject, immediately instruct the subject to "stop visualizing that, and go on relaxing." Then continue with suggestions of relaxation (at least one minute) until the subject reports as deep a relaxation as before. Then inform him that you will shorten the presentation so that anxiety will not occur. Then, present the same item again for a period of only 3 to 5 seconds. If anxiety is still aroused, drop back to a 10-second presentation of the previous item in the hierarchy. If, however, the 3- to 5-second presentation does not arouse anxiety, give 30 to 45 seconds of relaxation suggestions, and present the same item again for 5 seconds, then 10 seconds, then 20 seconds. If the item can be presented for 20 seconds, move on to the next item in the hierarchy.

It is precisely at these points that clinical sensitivity must guide the presentations; one must know when to go back, when to construct new items, and when to move on up the hierarchy. However, the above guides should handle most situations. Some items may require as many as 8 to 12 presentations of differing time intervals, with lower level items interspersed. Most items will be handled successfully in 2 to 4 presentations.

Never end a session with a presentation that arouses anxiety. Approximately 5 to 10 minutes before the end of a session, either stop with a successful item, or go back to the previous item in the hierarchy. "Awaken" the subject, and discuss the session with him, reassuring him about any difficulties that may have come up. If by some quirk any of the presentations are nullified, or they do not carry over into real life, rapidly repeat those items in the next session. Normally, each session will begin with a single presentation of the last successfully completed item.

All subjects should easily complete the hierarchy in the five sessions. However, if any subject does not complete the hierarchy, take note of the number of items still to be covered, so this fact may be taken into account in evaluation. As many as six of the easier items may be covered in the second session, and only one or two items in later sessions; however, be sure to keep a record for each subject so that the proper items are covered.

E. Attention-Placebo Treatment Manual

This "treatment" serves as a control for a number of factors in psychotherapy. Hopefully it will allow us to determine the extent of the effect of these factors so that we can refine or use them in other treatments. The prime factors of interest are: the subject's expectation of relief; the attention, warmth, and interest of the therapist; and the subject's confidence in the therapist. Therefore, this treatment will be geared to include these factors, and to exclude any other basis of therapeutic influence.

There are four major procedures to be followed for this "treatment": (1) exploration of history and current status; (2) explanation of rationale; (3) administration of placebo; and (4) "stress training." These procedures are designed to be impressive and time-filling, but should be carried out systematically, both for ease of application and for comparability across therapists.

For the purposes of this research, it is absolutely essential that the therapist be as warm and as interested as he would be in any helping relationship, and that he maintain "confidence" in the procedures, while allowing no other therapeutic elements to enter. The therapist should always be positive in approach.

The following time schedule should be followed as closely as possible.

First session:

1. Exploration of history and current status (5–10 minutes).
2. Explanation of rationale and course of treatment (5–10 minutes).
3. Administration of placebo ("reduced dosage") (10 minutes).
4. Present "stress training" tape (fill the period).
5. Discuss reactions to "stress training" and "tranquilizer" (5 minutes).

Second to fifth sessions:

1. Answer questions if they arise (2–10 minutes).
2. Administer placebo ("full dosage") (10 minutes).
3. Present "stress training tape" (rest of period).

SPECIFIC PROCEDURES

1. *Exploration of history and current status.* This procedure will be relatively short, serving primarily as an "icebreaker" and as a period in which to establish rapport. Therapists should determine (a) *how long* the subject has experienced performance anxiety, (b) to what *degree* performance anxiety interferes with functioning, and (c) whether other social or evaluative situations also arouse anxiety. This information will be useful in describing subjects. Additionally, ask the subject if he has now or has ever had any physical problems, checking specifically on heart trouble and high blood pressure. The *only* purpose of this question is to add credence to the use of the "tranquilizer." If any subject should respond positively, reassure him that this will pose no problem for the present treatment. This phase should be completed in no more than 10 minutes of the first session.

2. *Explanation of rationale and course of treatment.* Here, it is most important that the therapist appear positive and confident. Each subject should accept the treatment process. Both the "theory" and the course of treatment should be briefly explained and repeated if questions arise. It should be emphasized that the "treatment" is a learning process. If any subject seems to have trouble "understanding," attempt to allay his doubts by telling him that he will see how things work as treatment progresses.

The following "rationale" should be presented (not read) to each subject as convincingly as possible: "The emotional reactions which you experience are a result of your previous experience with people and situations—oftentimes leading to feelings of anxiety or tenseness that are really inappropriate. Generally, these reactions are like those engendered by any stressful situation, and your body reacts in such a way to prepare you for either 'fight' or 'flight,' as it has been called. When your body reacts in this way, you can also become flustered or muddled mentally—in fact, these are reciprocal processes. Since these reactions, like the ones you experience in connection with speeches, are largely the result of a low tolerance for this kind of stress, we can work to overcome these reactions right here in the office by training you to work and think effectively under stress.

"The specific technique we will be using is called stress training. This technique uses two main procedures—tranquilization and counterconditioning—to reduce your anxiety by increasing your ability to function under stress.

"Dr. Young from the University Health Service has authorized us to use a newly developed and thoroughly tested tranquilizer for this training. Of course, many tranquilizers are on the market to help people relieve tensions, but these often have unpleasant side effects, and tend to become crutches for people to lean on. This new tranquilizer is not on the market yet, but it is especially good for our purposes because it has no side effects whatever. However, even in large doses, the effects of this drug do not last more than 40 to 45 minutes; therefore, by itself it is not very useful.

"We will administer this drug right here in the office; and while you are 'tranquilized,' have you work at a normally stressful task. Since you will be under the effect of the tranquilizer—feeling generally relaxed—you will not experience the tenseness or anxiety you would ordinarily feel working at the task. As you go through this repeatedly, your mind and body will gradually come to develop a tolerance for stress, so that you no longer become anxious in stressful situations such as giving speeches, even without the tranquilizer.

"The actual task you will be performing is one used in a government project for stress training of astronauts. We have obtained copies of the actual tapes used in this training. These tapes contain recordings of numerous sonar signals, plus a disaster or 'target signal.' You will listen to the tape over headphones and attempt to discriminate the 'target signal' from the others. Normally, the combination of difficult discrimination and the sounds themselves is very stressful and arouses a great deal of anxiety. However, since you will only listen to this tape while under the effects of the tranquilizer, you will experience little or no anxiety, and may even get drowsy as treatment goes on.

"Most of these procedures will become clearer after we get into them, but do you have any questions before we get started?"

3. *Administration of the placebo.* Each therapist will be provided with a container of sodium-bicarbonate capsules. These capsules will serve as the "new tranquilizer." A pitcher, water glass, and penlight will also be provided.

For the first session, tell the subject that he is receiving a reduced dosage to make sure that the effects of the "tranquilizer" will be entirely dissipated before the end of the period. For sessions two to five, explain that full dosage is used. Administer the capsule and make sure the subject swallows it. Then ask him to sit back quietly in his chair, explaining that the drug takes about eight minutes to start "working." Also tell him that he will probably feel nothing except a mild relaxation as the drug takes effect, and that the drug will not dull alertness or have any other noticeable effects. The therapist will then leave the room, if possible, or at least busy himself at his desk so that no communication takes place during the next ten minutes. Then the therapist will return to the subject, and explain that he is going to check to see if the drug is operating.

Ask the subject how he feels—responding "fine." Then stand and pass the penlight twice across each pupil, explaining that you are checking his pupillary response, which should be somewhat slower when the drug has taken effect. Indicate that such is the case by murmuring "mmhmm." Next, take the subject's pulse, checking with your wristwatch, and again indicate the expected finding. Announce, "You're ready now."

4. *Presentation of "stress training" tape.* Each therapist will be provided with a "stress training" tape, consisting of a series of signals produced from a variable oscillator. One signal, called the "target" occurs four times in succession at the beginning of the tape, and thereafter at approximately five-minute intervals. A headset, to be connected to a tape recorder, will also be provided.

After announcing that the subject is ready, explain that: "This stress training tape will present a series of sonar signals. There is a 'target signal' which will be the first sound you hear; it occurs four times in succession so you may memorize the tone. After that, the target signal will occur occasionally at different time intervals. Each time you hear that signal, let me know by saying 'target.' Do you have any questions?" Then adjust the headset and volume, and start the tape machine. For the rest of the period merely sit observing the subject, appearing attentive, recording the number on the tape counter each time he signals "target."

Stop the tape approximately five minutes before the end of the period, and ask the subject how he felt while listening to the tape, and if he had any difficulty with the target, etc. Reassure him that he is doing well and that things are going as expected.

Again take the subject's pulse and flash the penlight across his pupils. Tell him that the effects of the drug have dissipated. Terminate the session, reassuring the subject that his anxiety will be reduced.

F. Mean Pre-Post Item Frequencies of the Timed Behavioral Checklist

TABLE F–1

Item[a]	Condition	Desensitization		Insight		Attention-Placebo		No-Treatment Control	
		Mean	SD	Mean	SD	Mean	SD	Mean	SD
(1)	Pre	.8	3.10	1.7	5.68	—	—	1.2	4.32
	Post	3.4	8.97	1.7	3.77	1.9	7.23	.1	.29
(2)	Pre	16.6	9.61	19.0	11.50	20.3	10.15	19.8	7.09
	Post	8.6	9.77	15.7	8.90	14.6	10.52	19.2	8.90
(3)	Pre	18.0	9.81	12.2	8.51	13.6	11.46	19.4	9.52
	Post	16.1	9.20	15.4	9.36	12.3	8.36	21.4	8.83
(4)	Pre	6.3	10.70	3.7	7.10	1.5	2.64	4.0	5.55
	Post	.1	.26	.2	.41	1.0	1.85	4.5	7.93
(5)	Pre	23.3	6.54	19.0	10.62	21.7	10.63	22.0	8.83
	Post	17.5	9.93	16.3	11.57	23.5	10.19	19.6	10.99
(6)	Pre	4.5	5.21	6.7	10.87	10.5	12.54	7.0	8.60
	Post	1.3	1.54	1.7	2.71	6.1	8.31	5.5	10.24
(7)	Pre	21.9	9.71	26.6	10.93	17.2	13.19	18.8	12.30
	Post	16.5	12.47	25.8	9.13	20.5	11.59	27.9	6.52
(8)	Pre	12.8	11.21	6.7	9.42	10.5	9.52	5.5	7.29
	Post	—	—	7.1	10.82	8.9	10.60	11.0	12.84
(9)	Pre	6.9	7.70	10.8	10.82	5.1	5.24	6.4	10.16
	Post	1.9	6.96	1.9	6.19	2.1	4.06	6.7	9.79
(10)	Pre	11.7	8.22	11.7	9.05	16.5	11.17	13.0	8.39
	Post	6.3	9.24	9.7	7.19	14.0	11.24	13.0	10.75
(11)	Pre	12.9	12.09	15.9	12.00	14.5	12.74	10.5	10.94
	Post	2.9	4.46	5.6	10.25	2.9	6.77	8.5	12.50
(12)	Pre	—	—	.9	1.77	—	—	.2	.85
	Post	.1	.52	—		—	—	—	—
(13)	Pre	2.1	2.89	2.9	4.14	2.1	4.05	3.8	6.65
	Post	1.1	2.43	4.3	9.49	4.1	5.73	4.9	9.19

NOTE: $N = 15$ for Desensitization, Insight, and Attention-Placebo; $N = 22$ for No-Treatment Control.

a Item numbers correspond to item order on the Behavioral Checklist, p. 109.

Table F–1 (cont.)

Item[a]	Condi-tion	Treatment							
		Desensi-tization		Insight		Attention-Placebo		No-Treatment Control	
		Mean	SD	Mean	SD	Mean	SD	Mean	SD
(14)	Pre	16.5	6.78	18.1	8.33	19.0	6.07	19.1	5.87
	Post	16.1	7.60	19.0	8.63	17.7	8.12	19.1	6.59
(15)	Pre	17.6	6.61	16.4	8.02	16.1	7.84	14.3	6.80
	Post	11.6	7.47	15.5	7.96	14.7	9.14	16.1	7.52
(16)	Pre	1.6	4.21	2.0	3.12	3.5	6.73	2.5	5.51
	Post	.8	1.52	2.1	3.54	3.8	4.13	.4	.96
(17)	Pre	5.1	4.57	5.8	6.62	9.3	10.34	9.2	8.91
	Post	2.8	5.32	1.1	2.58	3.3	3.54	7.0	9.46
(18)	Pre	4.8	5.94	2.9	5.77	3.3	5.12	6.6	8.62
	Post	.3	.62	.2	.77	1.1	4.13	1.4	2.46
(19)	Pre	4.7	4.73	4.3	5.79	5.6	7.19	3.3	3.95
	Post	.1	.26	3.4	6.67	.7	1.84	2.2	4.08
(20)	Pre	24.3	5.69	24.6	4.70	20.4	7.85	27.0	4.96
	Post	19.5	6.71	23.0	5.24	21.1	7.17	23.0	6.66

G. Prime Data on Performance-Anxiety Measures for Total Contact Sample

TABLE G–1

*Mean Performance-Anxiety Scores, Pretreatment
and Posttreatment, on Total Contact Sample*
(N = 67)

| | Measure | | | | | |
Condition	Pulse Rate	Palmar Sweat	Behavioral Checklist	Stress Anx. Diff.	PRCS	SR-Speech
Pretreatment						
Mean	88.9	20.9	212.2	77.2	21.0	46.6
SD	11.74	9.02	42.79	11.39	3.01	6.38
Posttreatment						
Mean	87.6	16.3	174.8	69.5	13.3	41.3
SD	9.58	12.29	48.04	10.61	5.97	8.05

NOTE: Groups I, D, AP, and TC comprise the total contact sample. See also Tables G–2 and G–3.

TABLE G–2

*Intercorrelations of Performance-Anxiety Scores at Pretreatment
and Posttreatment, on Total Contact Sample*
(N = 67)

	Pulse Rate	Palmar Sweat	Behavioral Checklist	Stress Anx. Diff.	PRCS	SR-Speech
						PRETREATMENT
Pulse Rate		—17	16	15	—08	—11
Palmar Sweat	15		—08	—02	00	34
Behavioral Checklist	—01	02		—03	13	—08
Stress Anx. Diff.	12	23	27		30	37
PRCS	03	07	41	50		52
SR-Speech	09	34	13	55	67	
	POSTTREATMENT					

NOTE: Plus signs and decimals omitted from table. $p = .05$ for $r = .20$; $p = .01$ for $r = .27$ (one-sided).

TABLE G–3

Correlations of Pretreatment with Posttreatment Performance-Anxiety Scores on Total Contact Sample (N = 67)

Pretreatment	Posttreatment					
	Pulse Rate	Palmar Sweat	Behavioral Checklist	Stress Anx. Diff.	PRCS	SR-Speech
Pulse Rate	*62*	—06	—05	17	—07	05
Palmar Sweat	—16	*46*	04	15	07	26
Behavioral Checklist	—09	—34	*37*	00	—05	—27
Stress Anx. Diff.	03	—03	—20	*54*	17	27
PRCS	—02	—04	09	28	*44*	19
SR-Speech	—04	26	—02	22	26	*38*

NOTE: Plus signs and decimals omitted from table. $p = .05$ for $r = .20$; $p = .01$ for $r = .27$ (one-sided).

H. Prime Correlations of Therapist and Subject Ratings with Performance-Anxiety Scores for Treated Subjects

TABLE H-1

Mean Performance-Anxiety Scores, Pretreatment and Posttreatment, for Treated Subjects (N = 45)

Condition	Pulse Rate	Palmar Sweat	Behavioral Checklist	Stress Anx. Diff.	PRCS	SR-Speech
Pretreatment						
Mean	88.9	20.8	211.5	78.5	20.7	46.9
SD	10.94	8.73	42.08	10.58	2.93	5.92
Posttreatment						
Mean	86.3	14.2	157.1	67.8	11.6	39.8
SD	8.99	8.70	39.33	9.10	5.19	6.77

NOTE: Groups I, D, and AP are the treated subjects. See also Tables H–2 and H–3.

TABLE H-2

Correlations of Subject and (Standardized) Therapist Ratings with Pre-treatment Performance-Anxiety Scores for Treated Subjects (N = 45)

Rating	Pulse Rate	Palmar Sweat	Behavioral Checklist	Stress Anx. Diff.	PRCS	SR-Speech
SUBJECT RATING						
1. Specific Improvement	19	−16	24	03	−05	−20
2. Other Improvement	08	−03	08	06	00	−14
3. Therapist Competence	17	−22	10	−11	03	−05
4. Therapist Likability	−01	−04	18	−14	−06	−02
THERAPIST RATING						
1. Specific Improvement	22	19	23	31	−14	15
2. Other Improvement	−16	22	−16	−02	15	29
3. Specific Prognosis	−16	02	−18	−02	−18	−09
4. Other Prognosis	−10	16	−22	−11	01	08
5. Subject Likability	−06	25	20	−16	10	10
6. Therapist Comfort	18	17	24	08	08	16
7. Pretreatment Confidence[a]	−03	27	17	−18	21	21

NOTE: Plus signs and decimals omitted from table. $p = .05$ for $r = .29$; $p = .01$ for $r = .38$ (two-sided).

a Not standardized.

TABLE H–3

Correlations of Subject and (Standardized) Therapist Ratings with Posttreatment Performance-Anxiety Scores for Treated Subjects
(N = 45)

| | Posttreatment Measure | | | | | |
Rating	Pulse Rate	Palmar Sweat	Behavioral Checklist	Stress Anx. Diff.	PRCS	SR-Speech
SUBJECT RATING						
1. Specific Improvement	31	07	−35	−37	−46	−41
2. Other Improvement	28	12	−15	−08	−27	−12
3. Therapist Competence	24	−12	−02	−19	−35	−20
4. Therapist Likability	−02	−07	20	−15	−24	−18
THERAPIST RATING						
1. Specific Improvement	09	08	−29	−12	−50	−21
2. Other Improvement	−27	13	08	02	29	29
3. Specific Prognosis	−15	06	43	32	42	30
4. Other Prognosis	−02	06	31	30	18	25
5. Subject Likability	−21	05	06	−12	−09	00
6. Therapist Comfort	05	−09	−26	−04	−06	−07
7. Pretreatment Confidence[a]	−10	04	04	03	16	18

NOTE: Plus signs and decimals omitted from table. $p = .05$ for $r = .29$; $p = .01$ for $r = .38$ (two-sided).
[a] Not standardized.

I. Test Battery Data on Total Sample

TABLE I-1

*Mean Test-Battery Scores, Pretreatment and at Follow-up, on
Total Sample Completing Speech Course (N = 92)*

Condition	Extro.-Intro.	Emot.	IPAT Anxiety	Anxiety Diff.	MMPI L	SR-Contest	SR-Interview	SR-Exam	SR-Speech	PRCS
Pretreatment										
Mean	15.8	18.7	37.1	64.2	2.4	36.0	36.4	40.9	46.0	20.6
SD	6.73	6.02	11.09	13.62	1.60	9.81	11.24	11.23	6.41	3.31
Follow-up										
Mean	18.5	17.8	35.4	64.3	2.4	35.9	34.7	40.9	41.6	14.4
SD	7.05	7.06	12.31	13.45	1.71	9.85	10.44	12.23	9.04	6.27

NOTE: The total sample is made up of all the groups: I, D, AP, TC, and CC. See also Tables I-2 and I-3.

TABLE I-2

Intercorrelations of Test-Battery Scales Administered at Pretreatment and at Follow-up on Total Sample Completing Speech Course (N = 92)

PRETREATMENT (upper right triangle) / FOLLOW-UP (lower left triangle)

Scale	Extro.-Intro.	Emot.	IPAT Anxiety	Anxiety Diff.	MMPI L	SR-Contest	SR-Interview	SR-Exam	SR-Speech	PRCS
Extro.-Intro.		02	−14	−16	05	01	−19	−07	−11	−16
Emotionality	−02		65	08	−19	21	18	30	12	−11
IPAT Anxiety	−07	73		18	−42	29	28	30	18	−02
Anxiety Diff.	10	50	49		−07	21	15	11	16	22
MMPI-L	02	−06	−21	01		−14	−22	−16	−28	−07
SR-Contest	11	49	46	45	−09		41	34	48	25
SR-Interview	−13	40	49	49	−17	57		59	52	35
SR-Exam	03	48	62	62	−19	62	68		40	50
SR-Speech	07	36	46	62	−01	64	60	74		50
PRCS	−03	25	27	44	−12	29	45	36	62	

NOTE: Plus signs and decimals omitted from table. $p = .05$ for $r = .20$; $p = .01$ for $r = .26$.

134

TABLE I–3

Correlations of Pretreatment with Follow-up Scales of the Test Battery on Total Sample Completing Speech Course (N = 92)

Pretreatment	Follow-up									
	Extro.-Intro.	Emot.	IPAT Anxiety	Anxiety Diff.	MMPI L	SR-Contest	SR-Interview	SR-Exam	SR-Speech	PRCS
Extro.-Intro.	80	03	−06	07	−09	13	−15	−02	00	01
Emotionality	−02	73	59	25	−10	36	30	36	18	07
IPAT Anxiety	−02	48	65	12	−16	25	26	31	11	−01
Anxiety Diff.	−14	13	14	24	03	07	27	03	05	07
MMPI-L	01	−09	−22	−04	44	−07	−11	−19	−03	04
SR-Contest	09	17	19	18	00	52	34	20	25	17
SR-Interview	−10	15	26	14	−04	22	56	24	15	22
SR-Exam	06	21	28	19	02	25	41	45	25	10
SR-Speech	04	−09	04	12	−07	13	24	10	25	26
PRCS	00	−22	−11	11	−10	01	24	05	09	32

NOTE: Plus signs and decimals omitted from table. $p = .05$ for $r = .20$; $p = .01$ for $r = .26$.

J. Test Battery Data on Total Population, Less Sample

TABLE J-1

Mean Test-Battery Scores, Pretreatment and Follow-up, on Total Population Completing Speech Course, Less Sample (N = 523 [341 males, 182 females])

Time	Extro.-Intro.	Emot.	IPAT Anxiety	Anxiety Diff.	MMPI L	SR-Contest	SR-Interview	SR-Exam	SR-Speech	PRCS
Pretreatment										
Mean	19.1	14.9	30.2	57.2	3.2	32.3	31.7	36.4	36.0	11.6
SD	6.27	6.49	11.01	11.28	1.96	8.52	8.65	9.89	8.31	5.90
Follow-up										
Mean	20.3	14.9	30.8	57.4	3.1	32.0	30.7	36.3	35.2	9.1
SD	6.20	6.81	11.54	11.88	2.05	8.83	8.73	10.11	8.65	5.56

TABLE J-2

Intercorrelations of Test-Battery Scales Administered at Pretreatment and at Follow-up on Total Population Completing Speech Course, Less Sample (N = 523)

Scale	Extro.-Intro.	Emot.	IPAT Anxiety	Anxiety Diff.	MMPI-L	SR-Contest	SR-Interview	SR-Exam	SR-Speech	PRCS
										PRETREATMENT
Extro.-Intro.		−14	−18	−26	−05	−25	−23	−08	−31	−31
Emotionality	−14		70	35	−24	29	29	33	23	24
IPAT Anxiety	−15	74		37	−36	38	41	40	34	32
Anxiety Diff.	−15	35	38		−06	24	27	24	30	36
MMPI-L	−06	−27	−33	−14		−13	−21	−16	−20	−13
SR-Contest	−20	31	38	29	−11		53	55	53	34
SR-Interview	−25	37	47	29	−21	54		55	58	39
SR-Exam	−10	41	48	41	−18	53	65		42	21
SR-Speech	−25	30	37	42	−15	65	59	57		72
PRCS	−24	34	40	42	−18	37	36	35	67	
FOLLOW-UP										

NOTE: Plus signs and decimals omitted from table. *p* = .05 for *r* = .09; *p* .01 for *r* = .11.

137

Correlations of Test-Battery Scales Administered at Pretreatment with Follow-up Scales on Total Population Completing Speech Course, Less Sample (N = 523)

Pretreatment	Follow-up									
	Extro.-Intro.	Emot.	Anxiety IPAT	Anxiety Diff.	MMPI L	SR-Contest	SR-Interview	SR-Exam	SR-Speech	PRCS
Extro.-Intro.	*77*	−09	−10	−14	−05	−16	−19	−06	−22	−18
Emotionality	−06	*77*	60	31	−23	24	28	32	22	23
IPAT Anxiety	−13	61	*74*	30	−33	25	38	36	29	31
Anxiety Diff.	−19	27	29	*43*	−07	21	26	26	31	32
MMPI-L	−07	−25	−27	−11	*65*	−07	−18	−14	−10	−11
SR-Contest	−18	25	32	18	−11	*60*	40	39	43	30
SR-Interview	−19	26	35	19	−14	34	*62*	42	41	30
SR-Exam	−01	26	34	27	−12	33	43	*63*	38	19
SR-Speech	−23	20	26	24	−14	38	42	36	*60*	50
PRCS	−20	18	25	26	−11	25	27	22	47	*61*

NOTE: Plus signs and decimals omitted from table. $p = .05$ for $r = .09$; $p .01$ for $r = .11$.

REFERENCES

REFERENCES

Bachrach, A. J., ed. (1962) *Experimental foundations of clinical psychology*. New York: Basic Books.

Bandura, A. (1956) Psychotherapists' anxiety level, self-insight, and psychotherapeutic competence. *J. abn. soc. Psychol.*, 52, 333–37.

———. (1961) Psychotherapy as a learning process. *Psychol. Bull.*, 58, 143–59.

———. *Principles of behavior modification.* New York: Holt, in press.

———, and R. H. Walters. (1963) *Social learning and personality development*. New York: Holt.

Barnes, T. J. (1961) An investigation of the relationships between personality traits and elements of speaking effectiveness. *Speech Monogr.*, 28, 71. (Abstract)

Becker, W. C. (1963) Consequences of different kinds of parental discipline. *Ann. Rev. child Develop.*, vol. 1.

Bendig, A. W. (1962) Pittsburgh scale of social extroversion-introversion and emotionality. *J. Psychol.*, 53, 199–210.

Bergin, A. E. (1963) The effects of psychotherapy: negative results revisited. *J. couns. Psychol.*, 10, 244–50.

Betz, B. J., and J. C. Whitehorn. (1956) The relationship of the therapist to the outcome of therapy in schizophrenia, in N. S. Kline, ed., *Psychiatric research reports*, 5. Washington, D.C.: Amer. Psychiat. Assoc.

Bookbinder, L. J. (1962) Simple conditioning vs. the dynamic approach to symptoms and symptom substitution: a reply to Yates. *Psychol. Rep.*, 10, 71–77.

Borgotta, E. F. (1959) The new principle of psychotherapy. *J. clin. Psychol.*, 15, 330–34.

Brenman, M., and M. M. Gill. (1947) *Hypnotherapy*. New York: International Univ. Press.

Brown, J. S. (1961) *The motivation of behavior*. New York: McGraw-Hill.

Bryant, D. C., and K. R. Wallace. (1960) *Fundamentals of public speaking.* New York: Appleton-Century-Crofts.

Cartwright, D. S. (1955) Effectiveness of psychotherapy: a critique of the spontaneous remission argument. *J. consult. Psychol., 2,* 290–96.

———, with W. L. Kirtner and D. W. Fiske. (1963) Method factors in changes associated with psychotherapy. *J. abn. soc. Psychol., 66,* 164–75.

Cattell, R. B. (1957) *The IPAT Anxiety Scale.* Champaign, Ill., Institute for Personality and Ability Testing.

Clevenger, T., Jr. (1959) A synthesis of experimental research in stage fright. *Quart. J. Speech, 45,* 134–45.

———, and T. R. King. (1961) A factor analysis of the visible symptoms of stage fright. *Speech Monogr., 28,* 296–98.

Colby, K. M. (1964) Psychotherapeutic process. *Ann. Rev. Psychol., 15,* 347–70.

Dollard, J., and N. E. Miller. (1950) *Personality and psychotherapy.* New York: McGraw-Hill.

Endler, N. S., with J. McV. Hunt and A. J. Rosenstein. (1962). An S-R inventory of anxiousness. *Psychol. Monogr., 76,* No. 536.

Eriksen, C. W. (1963) Perception and personality, in J. C. Wepman and R. W. Heine, eds., *Concepts of personality.* Chicago: Aldine.

———. Mechanisms of defense, in E. Borgotta and W. Lambert, eds., *Handbook of personality.* New York: Rand McNally, in preparation.

Eysenck, H. J. (1952) The effects of psychotherapy: an evaluation. *J. consult. Psychol., 16,* 319–24.

———. (1959) Learning theory and behavior therapy. *J. ment. Sci., 105,* 61–75.

———, ed. (1960) *Behavior therapy and the neuroses.* London: Pergamon.

———, ed. (1961a) *Handbook of abnormal psychology.* New York: Basic Books.

———. (1961b) The effects of psychotherapy, in H. J. Eysenck, ed., *Handbook of abnormal psychology.* New York: Basic Books.

———. (1961c) Classification and the problem of diagnosis, in H. J. Eysenck, ed., *Handbook of abnormal psychology.* New York: Basic Books.

———, ed. (1963) *Behaviour research and therapy: an international multi-disciplinary journal.* New York: Pergamon.

Fenichel, O. (1945) *The psychoanalytic theory of neuroses.* New York: Norton.

Frank, J. D. (1959a) Problems of controls in psychotherapy, in E. A. Rubinstein and M. B. Parloff, *Research in Psychotherapy.* Washington, D.C.: Amer. Psychol. Assoc.

———. (1959b) The dynamics of the psychotherapeutic relationship: determinants and effects of the therapist's influence. *Psychiatry, 22,* 17–40.

———. (1961) *Persuasion and healing.* Baltimore: Johns-Hopkins.

Franks, C. M. (1961) Conditioning and abnormal behavior, in H. J. Eysenck, ed., *Handbook of abnormal psychology.* New York: Basic Books.

———. (1963) Behavior therapy, the principles of conditioning and the treatment of the alcoholic. *Quart. J. stud. Alcohol. 24,* 511–29.

Gilkinson, H. (1942) Social fears as reported by students in college speech classes. *Speech Monogr., 9,* 141–60.

Goldstein, A. P. (1960) Patient's expectancies and non-specific therapy as a basis for (un) spontaneous remission. *J. clin. Psychol., 16,* 399–403.

———. (1962) *Therapist-patient expectancies in psychotherapy.* New York: Macmillan.

Goodstein, L. D. (1965) Behavior theoretical views of counseling, in B. Steffie, ed., *Theories of counseling.* New York: McGraw-Hill.

Grossberg, J. M. (1964) Behavior therapy: a review. *Psychol. Bull., 62,* 73–88.

Guthrie, E. R. (1938) *The psychology of human conflict.* New York: Harper.

Halio, J. L. (1963) Ph.D.'s and the oral examination. *J. higher Educ., 34,* 148–52.

Hathaway, S. R. (1948) Some considerations relative to nondirective counseling as therapy. *J. clin. Psychol., 4,* 226–31.

Heine, R. W. (1953) A comparison of patients' reports on psychotherapeutic experience with psychoanalytic, nondirective, and Adlerian therapists. *Amer. J. Psychother., 7,* 16–23.

Hilgard, E. R. (1956) *Theories of learning.* New York: Appleton-Century-Crofts.

Hinsie, L. E., and R. J. Campbell. (1960) *Psychiatric Dictionary.* New York: Oxford.

Hobbs, N. (1962) Sources of gain in psychotherapy. *Amer. Psychologist, 17,* 741–47.

Hovland, C. I., and I. L. Janis. (1959) *Personality and persuasability*. New Haven: Yale Univ. Press.

Hunt, J. McV. (1963) Motivation inherent in information processing and action, in O. J. Harvey, ed. *Motivation and social interaction: cognitive determinants*. New York: Ronald.

Husek, T. R., and S. Alexander. (1963) The effectiveness of the Anxiety Differential in examination stress situations. *Educ. psychol. Meas., 23*, 309–18.

Jacobson, E. (1938) *Progressive relaxation*. Chicago: Univ. Chicago Press.

James, W. (1915) *Talks to teachers and students*. New York: Holt.

Jones, M. C. (1924) A laboratory study of fear: the case of Peter. *J. genet. Psychol., 31*, 308–15.

Kalish, H. I. (1965) Behavior therapy, in B. B. Wolman, ed., *Handbook of clinical psychology*. New York: McGraw-Hill.

Kelly, G. A. (1955) *The psychology of personal constructs*. 2 vols. New York: Norton.

Kirk, S. A. (1962) *Educating exceptional children*. Boston: Houghton-Mifflin.

Krasner, L. (1955) The use of generalized reinforcers in psychotherapy research. *Psychol. Rep., 1*, 19–25.

———. (1962) The therapist as a social reinforcement machine, in H. H. Strupp and L. Luborsky, eds., *Research in psychotherapy, vol. 2*. Washington, D.C.: Amer. Psychol. Assoc.

———, and L. P. Ullmann. (1965) *Research in behavior modification*. New York: Holt.

Kuno, Y. (1956) *Human perspiration*. Springfield, Ill.: Chas. C Thomas.

Lacey, J. I. (1959) Psychophysiological approaches to the evaluation of psychotherapeutic process and outcome, in E. A. Rubinstein and M. B. Parloff, eds., *Research in psychotherapy*. Washington, D.C.: Amer. Psychol. Assoc.

Lang, P. J., and A. D. Lazovik. (1963) Experimental desensitization of a phobia. *J. abn. soc. Psychol., 66*, 519–25.

Lazarus, A. A. (1963) The results of behavior therapy in 126 cases of severe neuroses. *Behav. Res. Ther., 1*, 69–79.

———, and S. Rachman. (1960) The use of systematic desensitization in psychotherapy, in H. J. Eysenck, ed., *Behavior therapy and the neuroses*. London: Pergamon.

Lorr, M. (1962) Relation of treatment frequency and duration to psychotherapeutic outcome, in H. H. Strupp and L. Luborsky, eds., *Research in psychotherapy, vol. 2.* Washington, D.C.: Amer. Psychol. Assoc.

Luborsky, L. (1954) A note on Eysenck's article "The effects of psychotherapy: an evaluation." *Brit. J. Psychol., 45,* 129–31.

Marzolf, S. S. (1962) Fear and low productivity among superior students. *J. higher Educ., 33,* 255–59.

Mednick, S. A. (1958) A learning theory approach to research in schizophrenia. *Psychol. Bull., 55,* 316–27.

Miller, N. E. (1948) Studies of fear as an acquirable drive: I. Fear as motivation and fear-reduction as reinforcement in the learning of new responses. *J. exp. Psychol., 38,* 89–101.

———. (1959) Liberalization of basic S-R concepts: extension to conflict behavior, motivation and social learning, in S. Koch, ed., *Psychology: A study of a science.* Study 1, Vol. 2, New York: McGraw-Hill.

Mowrer, O. H. (1939) A stimulus-response analysis of anxiety and its role as a reinforcing agent. *Psychol. Rev., 46,* 553–66.

———. (1953) *Psychotherapy theory and research.* New York: Ronald.

Muench, G. (1964) The comparative effectivenes of long-term, short-term and interrupted psychotherapy. Paper presented at West. Psychol. Assoc., Portland, Ore., April 1964.

Murray, E. J. (1963a) Sociotropic-learning approach to psychotherapy, in P. Worchel and D. Byrne, eds., *Personality change.* New York: Wiley.

———. (1963b) Learning theory and psychotherapy: biotropic versus sociotropic approaches. *J. couns. Psychol., 10,* 250–55.

Osgood, C. E. (1953) *Method and theory in experimental psychology.* New York: Oxford.

Palmore, E., with H. L. Lennard and H. Hendin. (1959) Similarities of therapist and patient verbal behavior in psychotherapy. *Sociometry, 22,* 12–22.

Parloff, M. B. (1956) Some factors effecting the quality of therapeutic relationships. *J. abn. soc. Psychol., 52,* 5–10.

Pascal, G. R. (1947) The use of relaxation in short-term psychotherapy. *J. abn. soc. Psychol., 42,* 226–42.

Paul, G. L. (1964a) Modifications of systematic desensitization based on case study. Paper presented at West. Psychol. Assoc., Portland, Ore., April, 1964.

———. (1964b) A methodological note on the Palmar Sweat Index (PSI). *Psychonom. Sci., 1,* 264.

———, with C. W. Eriksen and L. G. Humphreys. (1962) Use of temperature stress with cool air reinforcement for human operant conditioning. *J. exp. Psychol., 64,* 329–35.

Platonov, K. (1959) *The word as a physiological and therapeutic factor: the theory and practice of psychotherapy according to I. P. Pavlov.,* Moscow: Foreign Lang. Pub. House.

Rachman, S. (1963) Introduction to behavior therapy. *Behav. Res. Ther., 1,* 3–15.

Roethlesberger, F. (1941) *Management and morale.* Cambridge: Harvard Univ. Press.

Rogers, C. R. (1951) *Client centered therapy.* Cambridge, Mass.: Riverside.

———. (1957) The necessary and sufficient conditions of therapeutic personality change. *J. consult. Psychol. 21,* 95–103.

Rosenthal, D. (1955) Changes in some moral values following psychotherapy. *J. consult. Psychol., 19,* 431–36.

———, and J. D. Frank. (1958) Psychotherapy and the placebo effect, in C. F. Reed, I. E. Alexander, and S. S. Tomkins, eds., *Psychopathology: a source book.* Cambridge: Harvard Univ. Press.

Rosenzweig, S. (1954) A transvaluation of psychotherapy: a reply to Hans Eysenck. *J. abn. soc. Psychol., 49,* 298–304.

Rotter, J. B. (1954) *Social learning and clinical psychology.* New York: Prentice-Hall.

Rubinstein, E. A., and M. B. Parloff, eds. (1959) *Research in psychotherapy.* Washington, D.C.: Amer. Psychol. Assoc.

Sapolsky, A. (1960) Effect of interpersonal relationships upon verbal conditioning. *J. abn. soc. Psychol., 60,* 241–46.

Shapiro, A. K. (1959) The placebo effect in the history of medical treatment: implications for psychiatry. *Amer. J. Psychiat., 116,* 298–304.

Shlien, J. M., with H. H. Mosak and R. Dreikurs. (1960) Effect of time limits: a comparison of client centered and Adlerian psychotherapy. *U. Chicago Lib. Counsel. Cent. Disc. Pap., 6,* No. 8.

Shoben, E. J., Jr. (1949) Psychotherapy as a problem in learning theory. *Psychol. Bull., 46,* 366–92.

————. (1963) The therapeutic object: men or machines? *J. couns. Psychol., 10,* 264–68.

Skinner, B. F. (1953) *Science and human behavior.* New York: Macmillan.

Snyder, W. U. (1962) Summary report: therapist's contribution, in H. H. Strupp and L. Luborsky, eds., *Research in psychotherapy, vol. 2.* Washington, D.C.: Amer. Psychol. Assoc.

Szasz, T. S. (1961) *The myth of mental illness.* New York: Hoeber-Harper.

Strupp, H. H. (1960) *Psychotherapists in action: explorations of the therapist's contribution to the treatment process.* New York: Grune & Stratton.

————. (1962a) Psychotherapy. *Ann. Rev. Psychol., 13,* 445–78.

————. (1962b) The therapist's contribution to the treatment process, in H. H. Strupp and L. Luborsky, eds., *Research in psychotherapy, vol. 2.* Washington, D.C.: Amer. Psychol. Assoc.

————, and L. Luborsky, eds. (1962) *Research in psychotherapy, vol. 2.* Washington, D.C.: Amer. Psychol. Assoc.

Sundland, D. M., and E. N. Barker. (1962) The orientations of psychotherapists. *J. consult. Psychol., 26,* 201–12.

Truax, C. B. (1963) Effective ingredients in psychotherapy: an approach to unraveling the patient-therapist interaction. *J. couns. Psychol., 10,* 256–63.

Ullmann, L. P., and L. Krasner, eds. (1965) *Case studies in behavior modification.* New York: Holt.

Watson, J. B., and R. Rayner. (1920) *Conditioned emotional reactions. J. exp. Psychol., 3,* 1–4.

Whitehorn, J. C. (1959) Goals of psychotherapy, in E. A. Rubinstein and M. B. Parloff, eds., *Research in psychotherapy.* Washington, D.C.: Amer. Psychol. Assoc.

Wilson, R. S. (1963) On behavior pathology. *Psychol. Bull., 60,* 130–46.

Windle, C. (1954) Test-retest effect on personality questionnaires. *Educ. psychol. Meas., 14,* 617–33.

————. (1955) Further studies of test-retest effect on personality questionnaires. *Educ. psychol. Meas., 15,* 246–53.

Wolf, S. (1959) The pharmacology of placebos. *Pharmacol. Rev., 11,* 689–704.

Wolpe, J. (1958) *Psychotherapy by reciprocal inhibition.* Stanford: Stanford Univ. Press.

———. (1961) The prognosis in unpsychoanalyzed recovery from neurosis. *Amer. J. Psychiat., 118,* 35–39.

———. (1962a) The experimental foundations of some new psychotherapeutic methods, in A. J. Bachrach, ed., *Experimental foundations of clinical psychology.* New York: Basic Books.

———. (1962b) Isolation of a conditioning procedure as the crucial psychotherapeutic factor: a case study. *J. nerv. ment. Dis., 134,* 316–29.

———, with A. Salter and L. J. Reyna. (1964) *The conditioning therapies.* New York: Holt.

Zax, M., and A. Klein. (1960) Measurement of personality and behavior changes following psychotherapy. *Psychol. Bull., 57,* 435–48.